WORSHIP IS FOR KIDS, TOO!

The Why and How of Children's Worship

by Ruth McRoberts Ward
with Foreword by Cal Guy, ThD.

Illustrative Concept by Jim Hooker

BAKER BOOK HOUSE
Grand Rapids, Michigan

All biblical quotations are taken from the King James Version unless otherwise noted.

Copyright 1976
Baker Book House Company
ISBN: 0-8010-9633-2

Second Printing, May 1980

Printed in the United States of America

To all our friends who wanted

"Sermons in a Sack"

ACKNOWLEDGEMENTS

What I have recorded has been derived from my actual experiences with children in worship. In a real sense the book was inspired by the children who were so enthusiastic and responsive to all our experiments.

I am indebted not only to all the teenage helpers of our church who have assisted faithfully these five years, but to all the members of Temple Baptist Church for their encouragement, assistance, and prayer. Especially faithful and hard working were Sue Plymire and Pat Miller.

Of the friends who were kind enough to read the text and offer suggestions, I am particularly grateful to Beryl Little, who gave me written evaluation and encouragement.

Last, but not least, my deep-felt gratitude goes to Jim, who as a loving husband and pastor gave me valuable suggestions. And to our four children —Kay, David, Julia Beth, and Roger—who not only assisted in worship but also prepared meals and did many of my household duties so I could type, I say, "Thank you."

Ruth Ward

FOREWORD

This book has been needed for a long time. It will probably be better received now than ever before because more people are realizing that the church must speak to today's generation in understandable terms. If it doesn't, much of its influence and following will be lost in the near future. This book starts at the right place to do just that. It gives helpful suggestions about how to make worship meaningful and directional in the lives of children and their families. It is not a book of games for children, but a book on how to communicate with them while sharing vital spiritual truths in the process.

Go back to your childhood impressions of church. Are they anything like some of the early ones in my life? The "card class" in Sunday School pushed us off behind a movable beaverboard partition and left us in the care of a stern maiden lady who filled my childish heart with terror of her, if not with fear of the Lord. Since my father was the preacher, I lived to pick up other impressions. But many people don't. Many don't get the next step because they drop out at the first one. Parents who most need the church will not force their children to go into uninteresting, unpleasant experiences.

Ruth Ward says it is not necessary for children to find church either uninteresting or unpleasant.

6

In sparkling language, she gives actual reporting of developments for children which minister to them and to their parents. In Pennsylvania, where Baptists don't gain members by inheritance, the church led by her husband, Jim Ward, has had consistent growth. Jim and Ruth are remarkable people, and this has helped in their acceptance by the community. In addition, this book recounts some fresh aspects of ministry that will help any church if used with spiritual insight and God's guidance.

The book is practical. It is factual. It bristles with ideas. And it meets an urgent need.

Try it. You'll like it. Better than that, your children and their parents will like it, too.

Cal Guy, ThD.
Professor of Missions
Southwestern Baptist Theological Seminary
Fort Worth, Texas

CONTENTS

8

WORSHIP IS FOR KIDS, TOO!

WHY A CHILDREN'S WORSHIP?

Perhaps you, like me, were never privileged to participate in a Children's Worship. Throughout childhood, I attended adult worship in several denominational churches. I learned to recite the Apostle's Creed and sing the Gloria Patri, Doxology, and Prayer responses. I loved music, so enjoyed singing the hymns even though I understood few of them.

During the sermon, however, I was lost. I counted light bulbs and ladies' hats, or played tic-tac-toe with my also-bored brother. Occasionally, a funny story would catch my interest. I was relieved when we didn't stay for worship. It just wasn't my favorite thing to do.

As was done to me, so we did to our four children. We expected them to sit in adult worship, reverently, while almost everything that went on was over their heads. There was one slight difference with our children, however. Their father was the minister, their mother the pianist. We never missed a service. They sat near the front where their conduct was scrutinized by all.

Many praised our children for being so good. But we coerced them to mind, as positively as we could, until they were afraid not to be quiet. They were not allowed to play, leave, or sleep. They may have been sitting down on the outside, but they were no doubt turning cartwheels on the inside. The cycle was complete. They felt as I had about worship—it was a necessary evil. They have survived, however, and all of them attend worship now because they sincerely want to.

Some people reason that the adult worship service is the place to teach a child discipline and reverence, a time when they can learn the old hymns and how to pray, and be assured of hearing God's Word preached accurately by a trained minister. The argument I've heard most often is that it is strengthening to a family to sit together in worship.

Certainly these goals are valid, but trying to achieve them in an adult setting often creates a few problems. Children stumble over the hard words and difficult tunes of many hymns, which speak, for the most part, about adult experiences foreign to them at their point in life. Unless a child is musically inclined, even the song service may be out of his reach.

Since most of the sermons are directed to adults, children can either sit quietly, their minds in neutral, or risk a thumped head, pinched arm, or threatening stares from their parents as they whisper for pencils and paper and something to do. Noisy "s-sh's" distract others, and occasionally a frustrated exit is made with ensuing spanking taking place on the way out. This puts a strain on worship. We have all observed smaller children being permitted to rummage through purses, registering delight at the discovery of keys, mirrors, and paper-wrapped candy. Everyone, especially the mother, sighs deeply if they magically fall asleep.

Needless to say, in the process of training children in the battle of boredom, much is lost. Not only does the parent suffer embarrassment and miss the thrust of the messages and depth of personal worship, but others are disturbed, including the pastor. Worst of all—the needs of the child are bypassed.

Some assume that sitting quietly through adult worship indicates that children are soaking it all in and learning respect for God. The fact is, they may be learning only patience and endurance, as well as developing a distaste for worship altogether. For some families, the worship hour is their worst hour.

How could this valuable hour be used to better advantage? Is virtue actually imparted to the child when he sits stoically through adult worship? If it's difficult for a minister to relate to adults who are on various levels of spiritual understanding, how much harder it is to reach children.

Many unchurched adults date their desire to stop attending church back to the time when they were bored in adult worship. Occasionally, people change churches because of the noise and disruption of undisciplined (bored) children in worship services. I think there's a better way. I believe the importance of worship is not so much quietness and solemnity as it is understanding who God is and how He values each person, including children, and desires to relate to them.

Let's assume that all churches recognize the value of providing teaching nurseries for babies through three years of age, and that we are dealing only with children four years and up. Some churches are forced to provide separate worship for children for various reasons, such as—

1. Lack of space in adult worship;
2. More children than adults in adult worship;
3. Presence of children without parents.

Other churches have tried children's worship and have become discouraged, because of—

1. Lack of workers;
2. Need for program ideas and methods;
3. Discipline problems;
4. Lack of space.

This book should offer encouragement in each of these areas. The ideas are based not on theory but on actual experience. Each program has been used with children from first through sixth grades. The principles of reaching children for worship on their level of understanding are the same no matter how extensive your outreach. The section on Teaching Methods and Guidelines goes into more detail.

Keeping one hundred or even ten children quiet is not synonymous with worship. Worship is fellowshipping with God, thus leading to a deeper understanding of Him. Our church was not forced to begin Children's Worship but chose to do so. I hope that the account on how it evolved will entice you not only to read the rest of the book, but to consider providing relevant worship experiences for your children.

THE CHILDREN'S WORSHIP IS BORN

My husband, Jim, was aware of children's boredom. Like many sensitive pastors, he incorporated a children's sermon in our service. He called it "Sermon in a Sack," a term he borrowed from an evangelist years ago.

He invited all the children to the front. Not only did this make them feel special, but they got to exercise their muscles right before the adult sermon. Giving hints about something in a sack, he let the children guess what it was. He would then draw spiritual meaning from the object or use it as a springboard for a story. These children loved the attention and learned that worship was not for adults only, but for them too. Many of Jim's original Sermon in a Sack ideas are included in this book.

Then one fall, about six four-year olds were "promoted" from the nursery to the adult worship service. Sermon-in-a-Sack time was not sufficient stimulation or sedation for them. During the adult sermon, they played, talked, cried, and made all kinds of noise. They made trips to the water fountain and the bathroom. "They need to be spanked," I heard an onlooker advise. "They've got to learn to sit still like ours did."

Anyone who has been around four-year olds knows they need to move almost constantly. Adult worship merely becomes a battleground—a contest of wills. Kids also know how to take advantage of embarrassed parents even though they bring toys, books, cookies—the works. Soon these mothers were spending most of the worship time out in the foyer. Then I noticed that they began to go home after Sunday School, and I heard comments like "I don't get anything out of it," and "I'll wait until Andy is a little older."

We all know that with time and training, an average four-year old can usually be taught to sit fairly still and occupy himself during adult worship. But the best behaved pre-schooler still gets restless, and the time is almost a total waste for him. It is fairly obvious that not much of adult worship is relevant to a child of any age.

After all our effort to get these young parents involved in worship, it tore at our hearts to see them drop out. So I began to ask the Lord what He wanted me to do. I knew already, but hated to think of missing Jim's sermons. And the question "Who would help me?" ran through my mind. Nevertheless, two weeks later, we began children's worship for four-year olds through second grade. I asked our own children—teenagers with much empathy for these kids—to assist. At first, not many adults were interested in helping, but they (particularly the mothers of the four-year olds) greatly appreciated the absence of the little children. Several older adults actually disapproved strongly because of the lost tradition of families sitting together in the service.

I searched old Bible School material and Sunday School teachers' books, raided the Sunday School picture files, and looked through religious books in our personal library for ideas. I recalled songs I had taught our own children. And I prayed.

Our first Sunday we had seventeen. Those first weeks we sang songs like "Jesus Loves Me," "Jesus Loves the Little Children," "Praise Him, All Ye Little Children," "Tell Me the Stories of Jesus," and action songs that had meaning they could understand like "Be Careful, Little Hands." We taught them choruses of some old hymns that had meaning for them, like "Blessed Be the Name," and "Oh, How I Love Jesus." My lessons and stories were short—all about Jesus, and illustrated with pictures or pantomime. I used simple tags for props: "Inn," "Stable," "Judea"; and tags for people: "Mary," "Joseph," and the like. The children always loved to wear name tags of any kind. We didn't copy the adult format but did something different each week, keeping it action-oriented and fun.

By the end of the hour they were tired, so we played "Beckoning," which occupied them wonderfully for the final ten minutes and also taught them to follow directions:

The leader sits in a chair at the front and points to someone. They exchange chairs and the new leader, sitting at the front, points to someone else. They exchange seats. This continues until all have become leader once. They must watch who has been chosen, for if the leader points to one who has already been a leader, that person shakes his head and another must be found. (This game automatically makes the children quiet.)

Other times we played Musical Chairs, or a quieter game called "Guess Who":

With the children's eyes closed, the leader describes something someone is wearing, like brown shoes. Everyone with brown shoes stands up—still with eyes closed. The leader goes further, describing brown pants. All girls sit down and only boys wearing brown pants remain. When the leader calls out yellow hair, a few more are eliminated. Again, "This person is sitting on the front row" takes out more. Finally, only one person remains, or someone guesses himself when there are only a few left. This game is not only a lot of fun, but teaches the children, if the leader so instructs, that God knows each of us. We are each unique and He loves all of us equally.

With the children out, the adult service was more conducive to real worship, and parents once more were staying after Sunday School. The children were having an enjoyable time—and so were the leaders. We were on our way!

THE CHILDREN'S WORSHIP GROWS UP

We noticed several third and fourth graders slipping in regularly to the Children's Worship. Some of their parents who were formerly irregular at worship began coming every week because their children didn't want to miss our service—even though it was geared to smaller children. (We have found that most parents will take their children where they want to go.) "Thank you for having Children's Worship," the mother of a third and a fourth grader said. "I get so much more out of worship now. I didn't realize how much the children disturbed me."

Six months later, our church began a bus ministry—just one bus. This added about seven to our

ALL ABOARD

group. But some of the older ones who attended the adult worship were so restless that often the ushers escorted them to our worship as a disciplinary measure. I realized that our service was not enough to challenge them in the way I'd like, and this bothered me. So I would slip in something on a fourth or fifth grade level from time to time.

Gradually our number increased to forty, many of them above second grade. I asked a different couple each week to take the pre-schoolers to a Sunday School room for the last thirty minutes where they made something, had stories, games, or special music; or talked about things pre-schoolers are interested in. That permitted me to gear some of the children's worship time to these older children who were at a decision-making age. I refer to the fourth and fifth graders rather than the first and second graders.

These couples were approached to try it one week at a time. If they enjoyed it, they could do it again in a couple of months. Many chose to repeat, whereas others were glad when their one week was over—once was enough!

A move into rented quarters while we were building initiated another change. There would be no room in adult worship for any children under twelve so we would have about sixty-five from four to twelve years of age in one service. This simply would not work. I would have to raise the level of teaching to keep the sixth graders from being bored, since they had no choice about being there. One of the regular observers and one who had helped with the 'last thirty minutes plan' volunteered to become leader for the twenty pre-schoolers, taking with her a couple of trained teenage helpers. No room large enough for all of them was available, so we had to divide them into groups according to age and kindergarten experience. This meant we needed more adult helpers, so I sent a letter to every church member, then personally enlisted these couples. Never once did I receive a "no" answer. Working in this way took some enthusiastic coordination, but was most rewarding. It not only acquainted our entire membership with the needs of pre-schoolers, but also convinced those who helped of their hidden potential. This plan was used successfully for a year. The letter sent to each member read as follows:

Dear Friends,

Ever wonder what pre-schoolers do during the 10:45-11:45 worship hour? After an hour of Sunday School, children are hungry and tired, yet they have another hour to go. They need a relaxed, pleasant, yet meaningful worship time.

Pretend that you are a pre-schooler. What might you experience? For thirty minutes, Pat Miller and her able helpers would lead you in simple worship with songs, giving, birthday celebration, praise, and a story. There would possibly be juice and cookies for you too.

For the next thirty minutes, special guests would come into your room while Pat proceeded to the other group of pre-schoolers. During this time you might listen to Tom and Dot Adams play their instruments and talk with you about music. They might teach you a new song and perhaps allow you to try their instrument. Another day, a vivacious Kim and her husband, Joel, would have a very special mission story hour.

You would learn that games, though fun, have a dual purpose, as some mornings you would play "Beckoning" which teaches you to take turns, or sing "All Around the Mulberry Bush" which teaches you to enjoy routine and work. There are lots of other games to teach team spirit and cooperation. You would have fun during special feature time too.

Ever watched oil painting? Karen Woodyard would demonstrate this as she talked about colors. She'd have something for you to paint also.

Pat Hooker would like to teach you about butterflies and rocks. She's a nurse, too, and would tell you about your wonderful bodies, take your blood pressure, and let you listen to your heart.

You would hear flutes, trumpets, guitars, accordians, and other instruments. Some days you'd get to make something to carry home when the especially gifted Shues or Jowano-witches were there.

When the weather was nice, you'd get to take a walk. Sometimes a couple would talk with you about your baby brother or the day you moved or what you like to smell or hear or taste. We'd want to give you time to talk about these things.

Back to reality—if you'd be interested in joining with other adults in sharing the worship hour with our pre-school children every three or four months, let me know. Try it once. You'll not be obligated to do it again, but will certainly be privileged to participate again if you desire.

The Bible instructs us to "teach a child while he is young and when he gets older, he won't forget about it." That is what we're trying to do. Children are potential adults.

The opportunity we have is tremendous—let's make good use of it. Thank you for your cooperation.

Sincerely,
Ruth

THIRTY MINUTES WITH PRE-SCHOOLERS
The following list of ideas was attached to the letter sent to prospective workers:

CIRCLE GAMES:

Meow—Guess Who Meows: one is blindfolded until he recognizes a voice.

Button-Button: could be Verse-Verse in a thimble. When found, read it to them.

Who's Missing: all shut eyes while "it" tiptoes

24

out. Whoever guesses who is missing gets to choose next "it." (Truth to teach is that God knows all of us.)

Farmer in the Dell: (choosing others again).

Mulberry Bush: (enjoying jobs and responsibilities of life).

Jack in the Box: (following instructions).

Beckoning: "it" points to someone—they exchange seats. The one in leader's chair points to another. They exchange seats. This goes on until all have had a chance to be leader. If the leader points to someone who has already been chosen, that one shakes his head and the leader must choose another person. (Teaches following instructions.)

Heads and Shoulders, Knees and Toes: (exercise song about our wonderful bodies).

ACTION SONGS THEY KNOW:

Be Careful, Little Hands

I'm Too Young (marching song)

Hallelujah, Praise Ye the Lord

The Foolish Man (be sure to explain truth first)

If You're Happy and You Know It

Zacchaeus

OTHER SONGS THEY KNOW:

God Is So Good

Go Tell It On the Mountain

I Have the Joy, Joy, Joy, Joy

Praise Him, Praise Him

Jesus Loves the Little Children

Jesus Loves Me

My Best Friend is Jesus

GUESSING GAMES:

I see something: yellow, blue, etc.

I'm thinking of an: animal, fruit, vegetable, color, person in this room, etc. (Thank God for good minds.)

RELAY GAMES:

Divide into twos or threes—

carry beans on spoon or knife to destination
put balloons through legs

(Keep it low-key if you have them the first thirty minutes.) This type of game teaches team spirit.

RECOGNIZE BY SENSES:

Blindfolded, let them:

feel: fruit, vegetables, or other objects

taste: food, spices, etc.

smell: spices, fruit, soap, perfume, vinegar, etc.

hear: music, voices, other sounds (use record player or tape recorder.)

CONVERSATION:

What new thing has God allowed you to have or do?

What is your favorite food, song, story?

Tell me about your baby sister or brother.

What are you most thankful for?

What do you like best about summer, winter, or fall?

BOOKS:

Read or browse through books from library or

Sunday School room.

RECORDS:

Listen to many kinds of music for children. Let them march or do what the music suggests. Let them recognize certain instruments. (Thank God for beautiful music.)

Opportunities during these thirty minutes with pre-schoolers are limitless. Be creative. If you would like to make something from construction paper for them to take home, have it well planned. It needs to be pre-cut for some of them. They love to find pictures in magazines, so making montages is an excellent activity. These are posters made up of pictures all of the same thing —like animals, or birds, or flowers.

TEACHING FOR THE OLDER CHILD

With the pre-schoolers well taken care of, the level of learning in first through sixth grade worship could be raised. I put it on about the fourth grade level. This would at times lose the younger ones and bore the older ones, but would reach the greater part of the entire group. Programs in this book were used for that particular combination.

I believe that harm is done when children make decisions before they are old enough to make moral choices. Naturally, the age of understanding varies, depending on home training and individual rate of maturation. Some are ready at age six, others not until ten or eleven. I prefer to work with the children until they are aware of the claims of Christ on their lives and the significance of a decision.

We presented salvation on their level, but since first and second graders are easily influenced, we put no pressure on them to make a decision at that time. I encouraged anyone who wanted to ask Jesus to take control of his life to see me afterwards. Many did, but they were all from the older age group of fourth through sixth graders.

Since our number had grown so rapidly, we knew when we moved into our new building there would be room for pre-school and first through second grade worship only. Thus, the third through sixth graders would be thrust into adult worship, some of them for the first time. So we launched into an orientation program to prepare them for the adult service. I also began asking the Lord for someone to take first and second grade worship, since I preferred to stay with the older children.

We discussed conduct in worship through story and skit. The teenagers were more than happy to illustrate how some children and teenagers behave during adult worship. We pre-planned for them to misbehave while I told a story. They acted up by writing notes, whispering, looking through purses, chewing gum, eating candy, going to get drinks, etc. They did a bang-up job. The children caught on pretty quickly and admitted they were bothered by their disruptions during my story. We applied this to adult worship and how the adults would feel if a child moved around and played.

I told them why I wanted them all to sit together (there were forty of them) whether their parents were present or not. I preferred to be responsible because they knew I would not permit them to go out, look through purses, write notes, or whisper.

Next we dealt with the Lord's Supper. We studied the background as to when Jesus instituted it and why. I told them what was in the glasses and what kind of bread we used. We talked about the various meanings and ways of taking Communion in different churches, since many came from other church backgrounds. I let them share what they already knew and had experienced.

We again used our teenage helpers to show how some children, and even adults, act during the observance of the sacrament. While I was talking, pretending to be the pastor, the teenagers sat facing the group and acted out things I've seen happen in various churches. While some tipped their glasses to each other, others whispered back and forth, and some even rolled their bread into balls.

After that excercise, the teenagers play-acted again. This time they listened while the "minister" explained Communion; they prayed when it was time to pray, and appeared to worship during the observance. I showed them how to hold the cup in the palm of their hands so it wouldn't spill when they bowed their heads. We talked about what one could think about during the quiet time while the elements were being given out. Soon afterwards, we took our third through sixth graders to a morning observance of the Lord's Supper, and was I pleased with their conduct! (That little lesson benefited our teenagers too.)

We discussed the invitation time that we have at the close of every service when people are encouraged to make their decisions public if they wish. We talked about why it was disturbing for people to put their coats on then or even leave the service. We talked about the kinds of decisions people make.

I asked different leaders in the church to visit Children's Worship and tell what Jesus meant to them and how He helps them on the job or at home. They met the Sunday School Director, the Treasurer, the Pianist, several deacons, and other key people.

Baptism was next, since we baptize by immersion and often do it in our morning worship service. Some of the children had never even heard of it, let alone witnessed it. We based our discussion on the New Testament background of John the Baptist and Jesus' baptism, talking about how different churches regard baptism and why we believe as we do. We also talked about what church membership is and is not—along with the responsibilities of a church member.

HIDDEN POTENTIAL DISCOVERED

A young mother, after observing Children's Worship for about a year because she received ideas that helped her teach her Sunday School class, said she would like to try the first and second grade worship when we moved. She was such a shy person, I never would have thought she would even consider it. I wondered how she would handle such a big task. But I had asked the Lord for a laborer and evidently He was leading her to volunteer. We were to see in the weeks to come.

I asked her if she would be willing to tell a story the next week. "You mean in front of all the kids—even the teenagers?" was her reply. I told her she needed the practice and promised to help her find an easy story. I did find one from LITTLE VISITS WITH GOD (Concordia Publishing House). She asked if she could use dolls rather than simply stand up there all alone in front of so many children. That was fine with me.

Toward the middle of the week, she called to ask if she could use puppets. She was too nervous to be the center of attention. "We've never used puppets," I said, "but if you want to try it, I'm sure it would work." I began to have real reservations about her. I hadn't realized she was so timid. But as I waited for Sunday to come, I prayed for her—and had another story ready, just in case she didn't show up.

The next Sunday I was simply astounded to see a lovely puppet stage made out of a $1.00 cardboard divider. She had cut a window and had put a little curtain around it. She gave a marvelous story using puppets she had designed—her first attempt at any such project. The kids were so elated with her presentation that they clapped wildly—the first time that had ever happened. All this en-

ZIP & ZAP – REGULAR VISITORS

couraged her—and me—so much that she wanted to do another story the next week.

I gave her another simple story and that, too, went well. She had learned to make puppets from books at the public library and made new ones for new characters. This increased her puppet family to four. She said they even had their own personalities. She was on her way.

Then she wanted to give a story that would tie in with my orientation lessons. This was during the time of our study on baptism. She searched the books I had loaned her, but could not find a suitable story. "What shall I do?" she asked.

"Sometimes when you want to teach a certain thing, it's difficult to find just exactly the right story," I said, "so you write your own."

"Write one! Me?"

"It's not so hard."

"I've never written anything."

"Just decide what facts you want to teach, then write a conversation using these facts and put names with it."

I quizzed her on the facts she wanted to teach and what she based her ideas on.

"I'll try," she said.

She went to work and by the next Sunday, she was really excited. Her story, introducing a brand new puppet, was so well done, I nearly cried for joy and unbelief at the same time. In fact, it was so marvelous that I asked her to give it for the Sunday evening worship group. They, too, were amazed and pleased with her new-found talent and unusual courage. She said she shook like a leaf behind the divider but as long as no one could tell, she didn't mind.

THE CHILDREN'S WORSHIP COMES OF AGE

The older children were getting excited about being in adult worship. The time was drawing near, but I was relaxed, knowing that the leader for first and second graders was found. The older children were invited over to the adult service several times to present the special music. This gave the adults a little orientation, too, of how many children there were. Jim reminded them that many of these children would be coming into adult worship for the very first time and that Ruth might be calling on them to help with the children. Ruth did, too!

We were proud to watch the forty or more children put into practice all they had learned in orientation. Their conduct was exemplary. Many made public their previous decisions to trust Christ. But with all this background, they still became bored with much of adult worship, especially the hymns. Our preacher is easy to understand, but even so, his simplest terminology was over the heads of many of them.

We had difficulty with only two or three boys, so instead of putting them into our four pews, we allowed them to sit with understanding adults. The children smiled back at me when they saw adults whispering or putting on their coats before the benediction. Even so, the kids began to hound me about when we would start Children's Worship again. The church had purchased a mobile home and put it on the property for space for us but the first and second grade group had grown, as well as the fours and fives, and they needed that space too. So we were locked into adult worship for longer than we had planned. I was almost resigned to the situation, but promised the kids I'd pray about more space, and reminded them that they should pray too.

Gradually, I realized many kids were leaving after Sunday School—some with parents. The size of the bus crowd had dropped off, too. We didn't want to lose them from Sunday School, but they said it was because they didn't like adult worship. Parents simply were not willing to wrestle with them to stay.

We intensified our search and found marvelous space just seven minutes away from church in a fire hall—brand new and air-conditioned. We moved Sunday School classes for third through sixth graders to the new building, giving added space at the church for other growth. They stayed there for children's worship and were bused back in time to meet their families after the adult service. It worked!

It has been a happy experience and no real sacrifice on my part these few years to direct and lead Children's Worship. Our church has caught the vision of worship on a child's level. The young people who have assisted since the beginning not only have learned much about understanding children but have grown spiritually themselves and tasted early the delight of serving the Lord. They attend evening adult worship as I do. We are proud to say we minister to the whole child. That's one reason, we believe, that our bus ministry is constant. We don't have to keep discovering new riders every week or give lavish prizes to fill our buses.

Children's Worship not only provides relevant worship for a child but allows him to be an integral part of that worship. At the same time, it releases parents to worship uninhibited on their level and participate in that worship by singing in the choir and taking part in other such activities. Occasionally, the third through sixth graders present special music for the adult worship and the minister preaches a sermon they can relate to.

From the beginning, our church gave its approval to Children's Worship by voting on it first and then electing me as Children's Worship Director. This placed me on the church council as well

CHILDREN PARTICIPATE

as on other key committees. It was also put in the church budget and given the monthly allotment I thought we needed. $10.00 a month has amply covered expenses.

My desire is to encourage all churches, no matter how small or large, to provide for their Children's Worship needs. Next, I want to inspire a director to think up his own stories or Sermons in a Sack, and learn to adapt Bible lessons to his particular group. This is not as hard as it sounds. Starter ideas are given later on in this book.

I write this book not as an end in itself, but as a means to this end. Like timid Sue in our church, anyone who has a desire to be used and a willingness to learn can do whatever the Lord indicates. A leader needs to have mature understanding about how God values each person and what the Bible says about sin, love, guilt, forgiveness, and salvation. But most of all, a leader needs to love children and really care about them and their relationship to God.

ENLISTMENT OF LEADERS AND HELPERS

Teenagers are excellent assistants because children idolize them. Invite teenagers who play an instrument or sing to have special music in Children's Worship. After they have experienced a session, they may feel inclined to help regularly. Let them observe several Sundays before asking

TEENAGERS HELP WITH MUSIC

them to commit themselves. We have five regulars who started this way. It's difficult to get anyone excited about a program he or she hasn't witnessed.

Teenagers take charge of the offering, visitor-welcome, birthday celebration, and "Who Am I" games. They also lead our singing and occasionally tell a story. They have chosen special jobs which they particularly enjoy—like taking coats, comforting a frightened child, tagging visitors, taking attendance, holding song sheets, arranging chairs. They have learned to involve a bored child by asking him to 'help.'

A leader needs to be firm but not harshly so. The ability to keep thirty or fifty children quiet for an hour does not necessarily qualify one to be a leader. Many factors are involved, not the least of which is a genuine interest in children and what interests them.

When we needed assistants for Pre-School Children's Worship, we asked the Lord for helpers first, according to Matthew 9:38:

> *"Pray ye therefore the Lord of the harvest, that He will send forth labourers into His harvest."*

The need can be made known by the pastor in the adult worship service or through weekly bulletins and newsletters.

Many persons who could qualify as leaders need encouragement and confidence. Children's Worship provides an excellent opportunity for spiritual growth for any who will give themselves wholeheartedly.

TEACHING METHODS AND GUIDELINES

The principles of life that we teach in church and Sunday School—like truth, courage, faith, trust, and forgiveness—are abstract ideas. It is necessary to liken what a child already knows to the abstract idea of what you want him to know, feel, and do. We must meet a child where he is mentally—the known—and take him to the projected spiritual destination—the unknown. Choosing the vehicle, or method, that will transport the child the quickest and most effective way requires insight. Using the same method all the time, say sermonlike lessons, becomes boring to him. Variety in Children's Worship is the answer to good teaching and good discipline, and assures pleasant learning.

Laws of psychology teach us that we seldom forget anything we learn with pleasure. But getting children interested in abstract ideas based on characters who lived thousands of years ago is especially difficult. It takes the skillful use of various methods and tools. Stories are the most common vehicle used to take children from the known to the unknown. Sermons in a Sack, montages, and pantomime may take a little more preparation, but can be very effective and are a welcome change for the children.

Some say that symbolism, like that used in object lessons, is a poor method of teaching. But I believe such lessons can be effective tools to reach into a child's mind if they are used well. Here are some examples of symbolism with meaning:

Give a flower to a child one petal at a time, explaining that this is how some people give themselves to God—just a little here and a little there. Then pull out another flower and hand it to the same child, saying that God wants the whole person—his voice, his talents, his mind, and all the rest.

Show three candles of different sizes. Ask which is the son, father, and grandfather. Then explain how the largest is the son because he has most of his life yet to live for God; the middle-size is the father, because he is half through; the shortest one is the grandfather. The point is, obviously, to give one's life to God while one has a lot of life to give.

It must be remembered that there is poor symbolism in using colors for hearts or a quality of life, or employing abstract ideas to teach abstract ideas. On the other hand, something as simple as tying string around a wrist to illustrate habits makes an impression. (Object lesson using string is found in section on Lesson Starter Suggestions.) We need to get their attention by starting with what they know or can see, and then proceed to our abstract or spiritual destination. These are two suggestions:

If the story is about the Good Samaritan, begin with where the child is. E.g., "Have you ever had a wreck on your bike? Did someone come to your aid?" Or "Has your father ever stopped to help an injured motorist?"

Begin the story about the woman with an issue of blood by asking how many have had chicken pox or something that kept them away from others. Or first tell a story about Jenny who was sad because no one would hold hands with her because she had warts.

Apart from being very familiar with the story, the most important aspects in good storytelling are eye contact and voice animation. Children sense when a teacher is unprepared—for instance, when he has to read the story. Mentioning the name of a restless child as you tell a story is an excellent way to keep or regain attention. Storytelling is an art that anyone can learn. The key is practice. No matter what method is used, friendliness is the most important attitude a teacher can have in addition to being a warm Christian. Lasting smiles teach lasting lessons.

Before using a pantomime or flannelboard story, the teacher must practice each scene by word and action, so he will know exactly where he will put every picture and sign. In choosing characters for a pantomime, avoid picking a poor child to play the part of a poor person. Children tend to become the one they pantomime.

Good teaching involves good discipline. Occasionally, a child will lose interest and become bored through no fault of his own. He may have grown tired or hungry; or in trying to reach the older children you may have gone over the head of a younger one. Recapture his interest by asking him to hold a picture, or simply to stand by you rather than isolate or shame him.

Another point I have discovered is that children

are reached better through positive statements than
through negative ones. Saying "Chairs are for sitting" rather than "Don't put your feet on the
chairs," or "Running and yelling is for outdoors"
rather than "Don't run and shout in here" are more
likely to result in the desired response.

I have benefited from Hiam Ginott's BETWEEN
PARENT AND CHILD (paperback from most news-
stands) in learning to be positive and avoiding negative sarcasm. These are statements that sound
funny or good but have abusive intent: "Don't you
look pretty!" when a child is caught making faces;
or "You're such a fine example to the younger
children," when a fifth grader is making airplanes.

We use several different ways to teach Bible
verses, all of which are from modern translations
of the Bible. They can be written out on posters
for group reading (even the younger ones not able
to read well will learn from hearing). Ask different grades to read a verse; then cover key phrases
or words and ask them to read it again. Each time,
cover more words and phrases. They will soon
know it word-perfect.

Writing the verse on 5x7 cards by words or
phrases provides another way to review. Sometimes we give groups of four the same verse to
unscramble from these individual cards. This involves everyone. First and second graders are not
as ready for competition as third through sixth
graders, so allow them to watch and become involved as they wish.

The cards with phrases or words can be held by children (perhaps the younger ones) in scrambled form and a reader can attempt to place them in proper sequence. Or arrange cards in scrambled form on a strip chart and allow volunteers to straighten them out.

Bible games are also good for reviewing facts. We compiled our own "Who Am I?" game from lessons we have had. One method is to choose two girls to compete with two boys in front of

QUIZZES ARE POPULAR

the group. Naturally, the younger ones will enjoy watching rather than getting involved until they know the answers fairly well.

One popular game is asking questions to the whole group and giving the card to the one who answers correctly. He or she holds the card until the end of the game, when a count of cards is taken. Even the younger ones will try this. If space permits, divide the children into age groups for games geared to their particular abilities.

We want Children's Worship to be not only informative and worshipful, but pleasant and fun. The last few minutes of Children's Worship should be relaxed. After all, many of them will be completing more than two hours of sitting and learning. Informal dialog about a subject or even a circle or blindfold game is good teaching at that time, and interesting to all.

FORMAT FOR PRE-SCHOOL CHILDREN'S WORSHIP

Seating: In circle, preferably—encourages quiet— discourages chair-kicking; gives better eye contact.

Quiet Music: Sets the mood. Instrumental is excellent.

Prayer: Brief—by teacher.

Welcome: Arrange with Sunday School teachers to tag visitors with lapel pin or ribbon.

Welcome Song: "There's a Welcome Here" or similar one.

Birthdays: Use a bank shaped like a church in which each child having a birthday puts a penny for each year. (It's helpful to have a list of birth dates.)

Birthday Song: "Happy Birthday," inserting "God bless you and keep you."

Offering: One child, perhaps the birthday child, carries basket around circle. (Each child handling the basket is time-consuming and dropping is frequent.) We have used a "special chair" to determine who carries basket.

Prayer of Thanks: Teacher.

Song of Thanks: "Praise Him, Praise Him, All Ye Little Children" or similar one.

Story: Brief—using simple Sermon-in-a-Sack lesson, pantomime, picture posing, flannel-board, or the like. (See section on story telling.)

New Song: Should grow out of story theme. Use record or tape recorder if piano is not available. Autoharp is good. Be sure to explain any words they might not understand, like "weep."

Verse: Usually growing out of story. Portions of verses can be used. Using a rebus (pictures in place of key words) is a good way to teach verses or parts of verses, and for review.

Songs: Familiar, short, easily understood songs.

Special Feature: Use about thirty minutes in various activities. Older children or teenagers can play instruments or sing; have mission story; have nature study on rocks, flowers, bees, and so on; have visits from nurse, doctor, business man, or anyone who can share what Jesus means to him as he helps other people.

Pre-schoolers are very tired after spending an hour in Sunday School and another one in Children's Worship, so the atmosphere should be kept relaxed. Serving juice and cookies and having a brief rest time are helpful.

FORMAT FOR FIRST-SIXTH GRADE CHILDREN'S WORSHIP

Quiet Music: Heads bowed—prayer suggestions given, such as "Thank God for the person who brought you to church," or something similar.

Song: A familiar hymn or chorus of hymn with message they can understand and experience. See "About Singing" section for ideas.

Prayer: By helper or child, or occasionally, the Lord's Prayer.

Prayer Song: "Child's Morning Hymn" or similar song.

Scripture: Either write out on poster or use individual Bibles. An overhead projector is excellent for this activity.

Offering: Ushers chosen ahead of time—quiet attitude of worship taught. Prayer offered by a child.

Offertory: Played by one of the children or teenage helpers.

Expression of Praise: "Doxology," previously explained and sung for several Sundays. Or use another thank-you song such as "Praise Him."

Special Music: Provided by a child or teenage helper. Try to use every child who plays any instrument at school. Many are even willing to sing a song they have learned in Children's Worship. Children appreciate one another's talents.

Story-lesson: Presented in variety of ways: "Sermon in a Sack," pantomime, montage, flannelboard, story, puppets, visitors, movies, plays. (See ideas further on in the book.)

Song: Teach hymns or songs that grow out of story theme. Writing song on poster will help the children memorize it more quickly than using books. Also, posters eliminate a lot of confusion and noise.

Welcome Visitors: Present with lapel pin, ribbon, or pencil, after introduction.

Welcome Song: "There's a Welcome Here" or similar song.

Birthday Time: Use "church" bank to collect pennies that go to missions—one for every year of child's age. Children are proud when birthday time comes. Sing "Happy Birthday" using "God bless and keep you."

Verse Review: Group learning from poster; individual recitation or section recitation. Girls and boys compete with one another. (See suggestions further on in book.)

Relaxation time: Mission story, action songs, rounds, Bible games, discussion, favorite song time, review of previous verses, or additional special music. Fifteen minutes is ample time for this activity.

Closing Prayer: By leader.

We alter the format often. An example:

Music: To sit down and get settled—lively instrumental.

Songs: Choruses, action songs: "If you're happy

and you know it," "I have the joy," "Rejoice in the Lord Always."

Visitor/Birthdays: Recognition.

Song: "Blessed Be the Name," or the new song being taught.

Quiet Music: Instrumental (we use taped music). Meditation period.

Prayer: By leader.

Lord's Prayer: In unison.

Hymn: Tied in with theme.

Offering: Ushers chosen among children.

Scripture: Read from poster or Bible.

Story Lesson: Methods as described elsewhere in book.

Song: Also tied in with theme.

Verse Review: Game, strip chart-quiz (more relaxed time).

Closing Prayer: By leader.

This method puts the worship section in the middle with relaxed activities on either side, giving children a break between Sunday School and worship. Some churches serve refreshments then.

Seating arrangement: Arrange chairs according to any activity such as game, special guest, pantomime. Insist on even rows (if the children have to place chairs themselves) and uniform arrangement. Following are illustrations of seating arrangements we have used.

When we are going to have a quiz, we use this

arrangement with the helpers seated in the single row to assist:

For puppet or story lesson:

For special guest/musician/speaker, we use a semicircle in rows or a continuous semicircle:

ABOUT SINGING

The goal in Children's Worship is to sing meaningful songs, hymns, and choruses that the children can understand and enjoy. Lyrics to many delightful gospel songs and church hymns are over the children's heads spiritually. Always consider the words first. Sometimes a song will have meaningful lyrics but a very difficult tune; or it may be out of the voice range of children. "Give of Your Best to the Master" is an example. Children's voices are not necessarily pitched as high as the range of many hymns. A guitar or autoharp accompaniment in a lower key solves that problem.

There's no particular merit in loud singing. It

may, in fact, even over-excite the children and lead to a discipline problem. It is important to keep the children aware of the words by reminding them of the meaning.

We have found children's hymns and songs on records an easy and enjoyable way to teach a new song. The bookstores have many selections, such

HYMN BOOKS ARE NOT NEEDED

as 'sing along' records with instruments and voices. A balance selector makes it possible to hear only the music, or only the voice, or both.

Children enjoy singing rounds. Seating arrangements can be helpful to divide the children into groups for the different parts. We have used rounds and hymns from adults' and children's hymn books, old Sunday School hymnals, and chorus books. Some songs have been gleaned from camps through the years.

ADULTS' HYMNS that children can understand and enjoy:
This Is My Father's World
For the Beauty of the Earth
Blessed Be the Name
There Is a Name I Love to Hear

50

What a Friend We Have in Jesus
The Light of the World
Follow On
Trust and Obey
Open My Eyes
Take My Life
He Lives
Since Jesus Came Into My Heart
I Would Be True
Onward Christian Soldiers
All Creatures of Our God and King
Holy Bible, Book Divine
CHILDREN'S HYMNS:
Creation
This Is My Father's World
For the Beauty of the Earth
All Things Bright and Beautiful
Holy Bible, Book Divine
Jesus Loves Me
Jesus Loves the Little Children
The Bible Is the Best Book
Tell Me the Story of Jesus
God Speaks to Us in Things We Hear
Onward Christian Soldiers
Wonderful Words of Life
Go Tell It on the Mountain
CHORUSES:
Jesus In the Morning
They'll Know We Are Christians by Our Love
If You're Happy and You Know It
Be Careful, Little Hands (action song)

For God So Loved the World
God Is So Good
I Have the Joy, Joy, Joy, Joy
Oh, Say but I'm Glad
Hallelujah, Praise Ye the Lord (action song)
Zacchaeus (action sing)
I Have Decided to Follow Jesus
Holy, Holy, Holy, Holy
I'm in the Lord's Army (action song)
Oh, Somebody Touched Me
ROUNDS:
The Lord Is My Shepherd
Love, Love, Love, Love
Be Unto Others Kind and True
Rejoice in the Lord Alway
I've Got Peace Like a River

Butcher paper is better than poster board for printing songs because it can be turned easily. Newspaper holders, like those in libraries, are excellent for holding these sheets. Some libraries may have old ones they will give away. When in a pinch for paper, the classified section of newspapers can be used. It looks gray from a distance.

As mentioned earlier, we use an overhead projector. The room doesn't need to be completely dark; and the words can be directed to a wall, high enough for everyone to see. As you sing, it is easy to cover words and sentences to help the children memorize the song. I use a permanent magic marker rather than a grease pencil on the transparencies. Any mistake can be easily removed with finger nail polish remover. Overheads vary in cost and weight. Since I have to carry mine to and from rented facilities, we chose a light-weight model.

LESSON-STORY IDEAS FOR FIRST-SIXTH GRADE CHILDREN'S WORSHIP

These suggestions are to be inserted in either format at story or sermon time. They will need to be simplified or explained depending on the level of your group. These ideas are merely to stimulate the leader who will eventually write his own material.

It is ideal to grade children in worship much like Sunday School if at all possible. That is, keep first and second graders together, third through fourth graders, and so on. Unfortunately, lack of space often prevents this ideal situation from becoming a reality. When this has happened we found grouping first and second and third through sixth grades quite workable.

Each idea in these lesson-story suggestions has been used with the first-sixth grade setup. I have made notations where a particular age group will be missed because of the age span. The age level we aim for is about fourth grade. In some cases we have used the same approach more than one time. We know ideas will work if the leader will adapt to his own particular group. Most leaders have a tendency to give children too many ideas in one morning. Keep the theme simple but meaningful.

Lest anyone think these suggestions are written for pre-schoolers, I assure the reader that they definitely are not. Pre-schoolers are not ready for conflict situations since they have not yet developed to the level of making moral choices.

CREATION

Scripture: Genesis 1:1-31

Flannelboard (preferably dark blue background): There is action in this plan as children have something to listen for and a place to put the picture they hold. Even though ideas are above the heads of some of the younger ones, they will enjoy the activity.

Preparation: Paste bits of flannel on backs of pictures mounted on construction paper—sun, moon, several stars, several animals, insects, colorful birds, and a 'Tarzan' man. Pass these out to children with instructions to listen to the story for the proper time to put their pictures on the board. Choose a good reader to read from the Living Bible as a teacher changes scenes. Make comments during the scripture reading in your own words.

1st Day (or period of time): Genesis 1:1-5; Darkness (board left blue). After the scripture reading say something like "Darkness makes no difference to God. He said *'Let there be light.'* Light and darkness take turns." (Place white flannel on half.)

2nd Day: Genesis 1:6-8, Beautiful sky (use light blue strip on top half). Make any comments you feel will help children appreciate the beauty of the sky.

3rd Day: Genesis 1:9-13, Dry land and water— mountains (use green/blue and brown strip on bottom half). Say, "Everything is very quiet in the world," then elaborate as you wish.

4th Day: Genesis 1:14-19, Sun, moon, stars (place on dark blue). "Everything is still very quiet."

5th Day: Genesis 1:20-23, Moving in the water— fish, birds (children should be encouraged to place pictures in appropriate places). "Now there is music."

6th Day: Genesis 1:24-26, Movement on land— animals, snakes, insects, cattle (placed by children). Say, "Also on this sixth day, God created the most important being—man" (placed by child on land). "God made man so He would have someone to fellowship with and someone who could care for the lovely garden. God created man specially. He formed him from clay, then breathed life into his body. The Bible is the only book that tells how God made man. Man belongs to God because He made him. Everything God made He called Good."

7th Day: Genesis 2:1-3, God rested. "A day to worship is part of God's plan."

Suggested Songs to Teach: "This is My Father's World," "All Things Bright and Beautiful," "Creation," "For the Beauty of the Earth." (Choose only one.)

OUR WONDERFUL BODIES

Scripture: Psalm 139:14

(Third-sixth graders will understand this more readily than first and second graders. Each leader will need to elaborate on various ideas.)

Sermon in a Sack—Object: clock.

"This clock is much like a person. Can you name some ways?" (After hearing their observations, continue.) "It has 200 working parts. Its hands are very important. They get us to places either on time or late. Hands are very important to a child too. They do good things or bad things. They make beds, and help in many other ways. Others watch what our hands do."

(Ring alarm.) "This clock also makes noise, much like a child. It screams when it's time to get up and go. Parents hate to hear it too; often we pretend not to hear the alarm and put our heads under the pillow. Did you ever do that? The longer it rings, the louder it seems to get.

"Something inside us (our conscience) rings loud when we're thinking about cheating or lying or stealing. Sometimes we act like we don't hear it and go on and do the very thing we know we shouldn't.

"Like a person, a clock needs to be kept clean for good working. A dirty clock loses time and causes problems for its owner. Our thoughts, too, must be kept clean. The Bible says that in order to keep our thoughts clean, we must know Bible verses and choose our friends carefully. We can also keep our minds clean and sharp by being careful about what we read and what programs we watch on television.

"In a clock, the mainspring is very important. It must be kept wound. Our heart is our mainspring and we need to wind it up every day with prayer and Bible reading. It's a good help to children if parents read the Bible to them every day and pray. But if you can read, you can understand parts of the Bible by yourself.

"The Psalmist was impressed with how he was made. God has certainly made us more detailed than any other creature by giving us a mind.

"God wants to control our minds. It is right for you to come to worship and to Sunday School to learn about Jesus and how to keep your mainspring in good condition. We should keep our clocks in good shape, but we don't have to go to a special shop for cleaning or for repairs like a real clock does. Jesus never leaves us, so anytime we need help, He's right there."

Suggested Songs to Teach: "Let the Beauty of
Jesus Be Seen in Me," "Be Careful, Little Hands"
(action song).

THE FALL OF MAN

Scripture: Genesis 2:16-17, 3:1-19 (background for
teacher)

First and second graders may not comprehend
theological or spiritual content, but they will
relate certain television programs to obeying
their parents. Since it sounds unfair to children that God would put a forbidden tree within
easy reach of Adam and Eve, then punish them
so harshly for only eating a bit of fruit, this
story points out that it's not what they ate but
why they did it that angered and displeased God.

Story: Rudy was home first from school. How delighted he was to find a new television set in
the living room. "This is to help you and Judy
learn easier and for your enjoyment, too," his
father said. "You may watch programs A, B,
and C but do not watch program D. It will hurt
you. You would learn things which would not
help you. Mother and I will be back soon."

Judy came skipping home. Rudy was so excited as he quickly told her about the rules;
then he hurried out to deliver papers on
his route.

As Judy watched program A, a knock was

heard at the door. She was surprised to see Jasper, a new neighbor. "Come in," she said, "and see our new television."

"That's nice," he said, "but can't you get program D?" Judy told him the rules, but he said, "Program D is the best one. Your parents are afraid you'll learn something and be smarter than they are. It won't hurt you to watch Program D."

So Judy changed to Program D. She felt bad about it at first but then she settled down because it was interesting.

In a few minutes, Rudy came whistling up the walk. Immediately, Judy opened the door to tell him about Program D. "It's really a great program, Rudy," she insisted. Rudy wasn't sure, but he began to watch it too. In fact, they all watched the whole thing.

Hearing a car drive up they quickly switched to program B. Judy and Rudy hid behind the couch, and Jasper hid in the closet.

When Mother and Daddy came in, they were surprised to find the children gone. "Wonder where they are," Mother said. "The television is on," remarked Daddy. "Rudy! Judy!" he called. Then he saw a foot sticking out from behind the couch. "What in the world are you hiding for?" Daddy asked, rather loudly.

"Don't get mad," Rudy stammered. "Judy turned program D on while I was out on my route . . . and . . ."

"Yes, but it wasn't my idea," Judy interrupted.

"Jasper, our new neighbor, suggested it." Just then Jasper stepped out of the closet and hung his head.

"O.K., Jasper," Daddy said. "Unless you agree to respect the rules of our home you may not come or play with our children. Judy, you will have lots more hard work to do and neither of you will get to watch television anymore but will have to work for your information. Rudy, you will have to work every evening after your route is finished and, of course, the television will have to go back to the store." (Very exaggerated punishment for effect.)

Conversation: Whose fault was it? (Receive several suggestions.)

Read Scripture from The Living Bible now. "God loves us but wants us to obey, not like robots, but because we choose to. When we go our own way it actually hurts us rather than God. Eve did not trust God. Adam did not pass on God's instructions correctly. The Serpent questioned God.

"God created man to be perfect, but He gave us a free will which means we can make up our own minds about loving Him. He will not force anyone to obey Him but we hurt ourselves if we fail to obey. He knows what is best for us because He made us." (You may want to elaborate on obeying our parents but that puts two ideas out and is a bit heavy.)

Songs to Teach: "This is My Father's World," "Creation."

THE NAME OF JESUS

(This is a little above first and second graders, but they will begin to learn that each person must meet Christ personally. They *can* relate to loving Jesus' name.)

Scripture: Acts 4:12, Romans 10:13, 1 Timothy 2:5
  (memorize Acts 4:12 or 1 Timothy 2:5)

Word Association: "What do you think of when I say the following?" (Allow for oral responses.) "Hershey, Yamaha, Pepsi, Schwinn, Mattel, Corvette, Unitas, Namath, Graham, McDonald's...". (Pause after each word to give opportunity for response. Can substitute local names of businesses.)

"Names do mean something. If I wanted to borrow money from the bank would they loan it if I said I knew _____?" (Insert any child's name.) "Probably not. But if I knew a man who had a big account there, the loan manager

CHILDREN LOVE TO ANSWER QUESTIONS

would no doubt give me the money—that is, if that friend recommended me and said I was O.K. and could be trusted to pay it back.

"Yes, special friends are needed often. It's not enough just to know about them; they have to approve of you also.

"There is a special name in the Scripture everyone needs to know in order to get through to God. Anyone know what name that is? . . . 'Jesus' is right. First Timothy 2:5 says there is one God and one mediator, or way, between God and man, and that one is Christ Jesus. Jesus approved of us when He died on the cross for our sins. He will recommend us to God when He knows we want Him to do so.

"Every person must meet Christ for himself and become a personal friend. Do you know Him? If you would like to meet Him personally, talk with one of us afterwards."

Songs to Teach: "Blessed Be the Name" (first verse and chorus),

"There Is a Name I love to Hear" (first and second verses and chorus).

SALVATION

Scripture: John 1:12 (memorize)

Sermon in a Sack—Object: Membership card.

"In my sack today is a small card that many adults carry. Sometimes children have them too. (Allow time for a guess or two.) This card entitles the holder to many benefits like eating, swimming, golf . . . (Pause.) No one else can use it. When this person dies, it is null and void—or no good. Anyone know yet? . . . (A membership card).

"God, too, has a membership list. How does a person get a membership with God? If your father is a minister or your mother a Sunday School teacher, are you automatically a member of God's family? Many people believe they are, but the Bible tells us differently. We are born into Adam's family, not God's. When Adam and Eve disobeyed by going their own way in the Garden of Eden, everyone since then has had trouble obeying God. It is natural to want to go our own way. Even babies, who can't talk yet, want their own way.

"Now, how can we get into God's family? Can we buy a membership or even earn it by working? Some people try to, but the Bible tells us membership in God's family is a gift from God through Christ's death. He won't force us to love Jesus, but He gives us an opportunity or chance to accept Him as our Savior.

"It cost Jesus His life to purchase or buy our membership and He wants you to give yourself back to Him. Our membership in God's family is good even after we die. He promises us eternal life, or life forever. As we bow our heads, you may want to ask Jesus to come into your heart." (Continue according to your own discretion.)
Songs to Teach: "I Have Decided to Follow Jesus," or "For God So Loved the World."

THE ANGEL SPEAKS TO MARY AND JOSEPH

(To be used the Sunday before Christmas)

Scripture: Luke 1:26-57, Matthew 1:18-24
    (memorize John 3:16)

Pantomime: (silent acting with very few props while story is read or told).

Characters: Elisabeth, Mary, Gabriel, Joseph — all tagged.

Setting: Designate places with signs—Galilee, Judea.

Reader: Choose someone who reads well. Use The Living Bible.

Scene 1—Luke 1:26-38 — Gabriel stands before Mary.

Scene 2— Luke 1:39-45—Elisabeth's home—Judea.

Scene 3—Matthew 1:18—Joseph's home—Joseph alone — Galilee — Gabriel enters, verses 20-21; Gabriel exits, verses 22-24.

"God spoke to Mary and Joseph through an angel. They were both willing to obey even though they didn't understand everything. Mary could have doubted or even been angry. Joseph could have broken up with Mary, but he trusted God.

"God can speak to us, too. He speaks through the Bible, through prayer, and through other Christians. God may be saying something to you even today about wanting you to be a missionary, minister, teacher, or businessman. He speaks to all of us about being good representatives for Him. He has a way to let those who are listening know what He wants them to do."

PANTOMIME IS EASY

(Pantomime is not to be rehearsed for performance. It merely allows the children to feel that the Bible characters were real and helps keep their attention while the Bible is being read.)

Songs to Teach: Christmas carols about Mary.

THE BIRTH OF JESUS
(To be used on Christmas Sunday)

Scripture: Luke 2 (memorize John 3:16)

Pantomime:

Characters: Innkeeper, Mary, Joseph, shepherds, angel, Anna, Simeon—all tagged.

Setting: Inn, manger, hillside, Nazareth, Bethlehem, temple—signs showing location.

Reader: Reads slowly from The Living Bible.

Scene 1—Innkeeper, Mary, and Joseph—Luke 2:1-7.

Questions: Why wasn't there room in the inn?

(Usually, not many travelers.) Was the innkeeper mean? (He offered what he had—allow
time for responses.)

Scene 2—Manger—Mary, Joseph (with a doll rep-
resenting Jesus).

Sing: "Silent Night"—words printed on song
sheet.

Scene 3—Hillside—shepherds, angel—Luke 2:8-14.
Angel leaves—Luke 2:15.

Scene 4 — Manger — shepherds, Mary, Joseph —
Luke 2:16-20.

Sing: Christmas Carol—"The First Noel."

Scene 5—Temple—Anna, Simeon, Mary, Joseph—
Luke 2:21, 25-33, 36-38.

Scene 6—Back to Galilee—v. 39.

Questions: Why did God reveal His great news
to shepherds first? (They would most likely
believe. God doesn't like the rich or well edu-
cated any better than anyone else.)

Why did God arrange for Simeon and Anna
to be present when Mary and Joseph dedicated
Jesus? (To encourage Mary and Joseph as well
as fulfill the desire of these dedicated servants.)

Song to Teach: "Go Tell it on the Mountain."

THE WISE MEN'S VISIT

(To be used on the Sunday following Christmas)

Scripture: Matthew 2 (review John 3:16)
Pantomime:

Characters: Mary, Joseph, wise men, Herod, chief priests—all tagged.

Setting: Palace in Jerusalem, house in Bethlehem.

Reader: Characters take their places while Scripture is read.

Scene 1 — Palace — Matthew 2:1-8 — Herod, wise men, priests.

Scene 2 — House — Matthew 2:9 — Mary, Joseph, wise men (star over house).

Scene 3 — Dream — Matthew 2:12 — Wise men leave quickly.

Scene 4 — House in Bethlehem — Dream — Matthew 2:13-14 — Joseph.

Questions: Did Herod really want to worship Jesus? What would have happened if the wise men had returned to Herod?

"The wise men listened and obeyed God just as Joseph listened and obeyed. Learn to obey parents and those with authority over you like teachers and older persons; then, when God tells you to do something, it will be easy to obey Him.

"Sometimes God's plans move us slowly. Sometimes, however, His plans move us swiftly, like Joseph's experience.

"In verse 16 Herod was furious and very jealous of a new king being born. So he tried to kill this new king, Jesus, by ordering all babies up to two years old to be killed. But his plan failed, because Jesus was safe in Egypt where Joseph had taken Him and His mother, Mary."

Song to Teach: "Trust and Obey."

HEARING GOD

(Probably third and fourth graders would understand this better, but again, first and second graders will absorb something about the importance of church and Sunday School.)

Scripture: John 8:47

Object Lesson — Use radio.

(Turn the radio on . . . there is no sound.) Ask "Why is there no sound or music?" (Someone will ask if it is plugged in.) "Are you sure it will work if we plug it in?" (Wait for responses.) "Because the transmitter is working — stations are broadcasting. Until the radio is turned on, we hear nothing. Sound waves are present even though we can't see them.

"The radio is like the Bible, Sunday School, worship, and all the influences we have to help us follow Jesus. But we must decide to turn it on. In the same way, we must decide to trust Jesus and want to hear what He has to say.

"Now, we can turn the radio on loud or soft, depending on how serious we are about listening. (Demonstrate loud and soft.) Some people want only a soft background of music while they work around the house — just like some people who want a soft background of what Jesus says. They want law and order and hospitals and people to deal with them honestly, but that's all. They don't want to do much. They don't want to hear Jesus real loud. (Demonstrate a loud, clear station.)

"Sometimes we get static or two or three stations at a time. There are always a lot of other noises all around us like static saying 'You can do it by yourself'; or 'Why try? It won't work'; or 'Money is the important thing'; or 'Have fun while you are young.' All these strange and dangerous voices try to drown out what God wants to tell us. (Get double station or static.)

"If we get a clear station and turn the volume up high (demonstrate) then we can hear Him clearly. That means we'll go to hear His Word preached and pay attention to our Sunday School teachers and learn to read the Bible and pray. The Bible says:

"Anyone whose Father is God, listens gladly to the words of God" (John 8:47 TLB).

Song to Teach: "Thy Word Have I Hid in My Heart."

WE ARE WITNESSES—LIKE SALT

Scripture: Matthew 5:13 (memorize)

Object lesson: Use bowl of salt and one of sugar. (Let several volunteers taste one or the other but instruct them to say nothing. They will make it very evident which they choose.) "Which would you rather have? (The majority will choose sugar.) Let's talk about salt. Can you name the uses of salt?" (They will respond with several uses.)

1. Salt keeps food from spoiling.
2. It is used for healing.
3. Dogs can live only six months without salt.
4. It seasons food.
5. Pigeons can live only three months without salt.
6. Cattle cannot live without it, even with plush grass.

"Our bodies have a lot of salt in them. Put your tongue on your arm. What do you taste, sugar or salt? Suppose you cut your finger . . . all this salt stops and rushes to the wound to prevent blood poisoning.

"Jesus said in Matthew 5:13 that you are the 'salt of the earth.' (Read it.) What did He mean? Remember, salt heals and also makes things taste better. An example of our lives being salt is what happened to a girl named Jackie.

"Jackie woke up to a cold, drab morning. She dressed quickly and went downstairs where she heard Mother moaning about the rainy day and how she couldn't wash windows or work in the yard. The baby was crying because he was hungry. Dad stared down at his wet newspaper.

"Jackie remembered she was the salt of the earth and was supposed to heal situations by spreading cheer. So she brought the baby a toy and a couple cookies . Then she played with him for a minute until he stopped crying. She gave her mother help with the breakfast table and said something pleasant to her daddy. She began humming a cheerful chorus she had learned in Children's Worship and soon everyone seemed to forget what a gloomy day it was.

"If we want to be like Jesus, we will take every situation and try to make it happier or easier for someone. Children can cheer their parents with only a little effort.

"God needs us to be cheerful, friendly, helpful, loving, and generous. (Have these words printed with magic markers on poster strips and stick to blackboard or wall as you talk.)

"Bow your heads; I want you to think of some things before we pray. Can you think of some way you could cheer your mother or father? Some way you could help with a younger brother or sister? If you can think of a way you could be the salt of the earth as Jesus spoke about, raise your hand. Now, let's thank God for the opportunity to spread cheer."

Closing Prayer: By leader or teenage helper.
Song to Teach: "I Would Be Like Jesus."

HOW TO BECOME STRONG

Scripture: John 8:12 (memorize)
Sermon in a Sack—Object: Leaf and apple. Hints:
  "What is the largest food factory in the world, that works all the time, even holidays?"

(Give time between questions for responses and guesses.)

"In my sack today is part of this factory. It's green in the spring and turns colors in the fall. (They will know it by now.)

"Leaves manufacture food which makes fruit. (Show apple.) They also give us oxygen to breathe. Without trees, we, as well as all the animals, would starve. Look at all these little veins. They are tiny energy lines. Trees have pipelines that carry water in and out to every branch. Where do they get their strength? (Pause for response.) That's right. From the sun. Every tree allows each leaf on it to face the sun. Leaves work all the time.

"In some ways we're like a leaf, except that God lets us choose whether we'll face Him or not—

SERMON IN A SACK

that is, get energy from Him or not. Jesus says in John 8:12 that He is our light and energy. We receive strength from Him as long as we face (or talk to) Him.

"We give off the necessary spiritual oxygen that the people all around need to breathe. Our fruit is the beginning of another Christian or helping a weaker Christian. Before we can grow or produce good fruit, though, we need to be healthy leaves that receive lots of light and water.

"Reading the Bible and attending worship, as well as praying, help us become healthy leaves on God's trees that will produce fruit."
Song to Teach: "The Light of the World is Jesus."

KEY TO LIFE

(Younger children, first and second graders, are just beginning to learn that even though Jesus loves them, when they are old enough to understand Christ's claims on their lives they need to accept Him personally.)

Scripture: Revelation 3:20 (memorize)
Riddle: "What Am I?" (Pause after each clue.)

1. I cost little but am necessary. (They will have many guesses.)
2. Even though I'm silent, I am helpful.
3. The one job I have takes less than five seconds.
4. Though I'm very small, I can keep even strong men out.
5. I'm easily lost.
6. Lose me and you'll be out in the cold.
7. Even important and busy people will take time to search for me.
8. Use me and you'll be warm, happy, and

safe. (They will certainly have guessed the answer before they get to number eight, but read the clues even after they have guessed correctly.)

Display a poster-sized key with Jesus Christ written from left to right and Revelation 3:20 printed down the shank of the key.

"How many of you have a key to your house? There's another key we can all have. See if you can guess this one."

Riddle:

1. You don't have to be rich or older to have this key. (Pause.)

2. You get it by asking for it.

3. Some people know about it but refuse to take it.

4. Those who have it enjoy peace and have meaningful lives.

"What is this key? (Pause for responses.) Jesus is this key. He accepts anyone. He won't force anyone to receive Him. He will give happiness and peace and eternal life to all who will receive Him. He died so we would have this key to spiritual life."

Song to Teach: "My Best Friend is Jesus," or "Just As I Am," verses one and two.

GIFTS FROM JESUS

(Written by Trudy and Bob Jowanowitch—
members of Temple Baptist Church,
York, Pennsylvania.)

Scripture: Galatians 5:22

Skit: (This takes quite a bit of preparation, but it
is an example of what can be done for variety.
When it was presented in our Children's Worship, all the children sat spell-bound, including
the first and second graders, even though they
couldn't understand all the deep spiritual
meanings.)

Characters: Life-size public mail box (use large
boxes) and life-size wrapped package addressed
to Mr. I. M. Saved. These are to be worn with
only arms and legs showing. The boxes rest on
the heads of the actors. (We used adults—the
ones who wrote the skit.) With the help of a
flashlight, actors can read the script if it's pasted
to the inside of the box. Better yet is to ad lib
the conversation to make it real.

You could use smaller box-like puppets and allow
children to read the script.

Mail Box (standing on corner): "Well, it's almost
time for the mailman."

Package (rushing in): "Hi, kids. I wonder if you
could help me? I just got in and have to find
a mailbox, quick. Have you seen any around
here?"

MB: "Hey! Over this way."

P: "Oh, boy! Am I in luck! I *have* to get in the mail today."

MB: "Why such a rush?"

P: "I'm *very* important to the person I'm going to."

MB: "Important?"

P: "Oh, yes! You see here? (Point) . . . Mr. I. M. Saved. Well, he just decided to follow Jesus, and for *that* he gets me."

MB: "I've got bad news."

P: "What's that?"

MB: "I have only this little opening and you'll never fit in."

P: "Aw, me! Maybe we could try to shove me in or something."

MB: "O.K. Let's try (shuffle around trying to force entry). . . . Stop! Stop! It's no use. You're much too big! I've never seen a package as big as you!"

P: "No, you probably haven't but that's because of all the things I've got in here."

MB: "What do you mean? What things?"

P: "Well, let me explain. When somebody asks Jesus to come and live in his heart, He sends him lots of things to make his life a lot better."

MB: "Like what?"

P: "Oh, my. Let me see what I can find in here to tell you about. (Pause.) Well, here's love. Jesus fills up his heart with love for every-body . . . even those people he doesn't like too well. He helps him see good things in everyone. He makes it easier to love his little brother and sister too."

MB: "What else is there?"

P: "Hmmm, here's honesty, because Jesus wants us always to tell the truth, no matter what. Of course, that means no cheating on tests or stealing either. Help is in here."

MB: "Boy! You do have a lot in there."

P: "Oh, there's more. Lots more. Here are patience and understanding. People always need these two things to get along with others. It's so hard to be patient with little brothers and sisters who cry for their own way or always seem to follow you around. And it's really good for the times they get into your room and mess things up. They don't mean to bother you, though. Patience and understanding also help you to share and be helpful."

MB: "This person you talk about must really be happy."

P: "Yes, he is. Happiness takes up a lot of room in here too."

MB: "Well, listen, you'll never get in here but I will be glad to hold your hand until the mail truck comes. I wouldn't want you to be late arriving to Mr. I. M. Saved, either."

(Mailbox and Package join hands.)

Director needs to emphasize that Jesus doesn't

force a person to be kind and caring; neither are these virtues automatic, but Jesus is ready to help a new Christian to be more like Him.
Songs to Teach: "I've Got Peace Like a River," and chorus of "I Would be True."

SHARING WITH JESUS

Scripture: John 6:1-13

Monologue—Object Lesson combination:
Write "SHARING" on blackboard in scrambled form.

"I brought an apple today and am so hungry for it (look over crowd). Oops! There's not enough for everyone. It's pretty big, though. I'd like to eat it now. Guess I should wait until later . . . or I could go right ahead and eat it in front of all these children. Or I could share little pieces with each one. But it wouldn't go very far and it's not nice to eat in front of people. I think I'll hide it before someone wants it.

"There's a story in the Bible about a little boy who had this same problem. His was the only lunch in a crowd at lunchtime. Maybe he tried to hide it, too, but Andrew saw it and asked him if he would share his lunch with Jesus. There were five loaves (like rolls) and two fishes in it. Let's have three boys act this out while

I read the story from The Living Bible." (Choose older boys.)

Characters: Jesus, Andrew, and little boy—tagged. (Movements will be suggested as scripture is read.)

Reader: John 6:1-13—read from The Living Bible very slowly with pantomime.

PLAYACTING BECOMES MEANINGFUL

Director now says, "I'm a newspaper reporter, and before you leave, little boy, I'd like to find out exactly what happened on the hillside today." (Spontaneously interview the boy who pantomimed this part.)

"What did Mr. Andrew say to you? . . . Why did you bring your lunch in the first place? . . . Did you want to give your lunch to him? . . . What did Jesus do with it and what do you think He is like?"

Discussion: "What can we share today with Jesus?" (Little boy can be seated.) As the children name things, write on blackboard: errand running, giving money, assisting others, and so on.

"We can do a lot of things for others, but *why* do we do them? Was the boy trying to make friends? Was he afraid not to share his lunch? (Their comments will be varied.)

"The only real reason to share and to help is because we love and trust Jesus. We want to be as much like Him as possible."

Songs to Teach: "I Would Be Like Jesus," or "Take My Life."

SALVATION

Scripture: John 4:14

Object Lesson: Use a very wilted plant.

"What is wrong with this plant? (Suggestions will be offered that it needs water.) Yes, it does need water very badly. In fact, it may be too late. It's been several days since it has had a drink. Now, if we water this plant in time, before it dies, it will begin to sprout and look very lovely like this one. (Display another well-cared for plant.)

"How many of you get thirsty at school? Sometimes we feel that if we don't get a drink in the next five minutes we'll die. We must have water in order to survive.

"Jesus talked about water to the woman who was drawing water from the well in Samaria. He asked her for a drink, then offered to give her some water that would keep her from getting thirsty ever again. What did He mean, I wonder? (Read Scripture.) He knew she was lonely and ashamed and had no friends.

"Jesus was talking about spiritual water. When parents don't teach their children to depend on God, they may go many years into adulthood before they realize how dry and wilted they are—like this plant. Unless they get the spiritual water of life—learn how Jesus can help them—they will be very droopy and lifeless.

"Jesus can help us to be kind and care for others. He can help us not to steal and cheat and lie. This will make us have a better life and help us be like a well-watered plant that stands straight.

"Jesus told that to the woman at the well, and she believed Him enough to go and tell her neighbors. Once we are acquainted with Jesus and hear what He has to say in the Bible, we too will experience this never-ending supply of spiritual water and we'll want to share it with others.

"This plant has no choice about receiving water. We water it when we get ready. But a person can choose not to open up to Jesus and receive the spiritual water He has to offer. This is sad—He has so much to give. If you have been thinking about how much you need Jesus every day and you would like to accept Him today, tell us about it." (Close in your own way.)

Song to Teach: "I Need Jesus."

DIFFICULTIES HELP US

Scripture: Romans 8:28 (memorize)

Object lesson (choose several volunteers to blindfold):

"I'm going to give you each a tiny taste of several things that you will recognize immediately. After everyone has tasted, we'll ask you what it was, but don't tell until we ask you. You can have your own private spoon and the taste will be very tiny." (Have ingredients in unmarked containers so the others will be in suspense too.) Go down the line and give little tastes of the following:

1. vinegar 3. water 5. oil 7. cocoa 9. vanilla
2. sugar 4. salt 6. soda 8. flour

(The children remain blindfolded.) "Most of these tasted flat or bad, didn't they? I wonder if they'd taste any better all mixed together? (Give each a generous spoonful of chocolate cake . . . they will register their delight. Remove blindfolds and let them return to their seats.)

"Each ingredient alone didn't taste so good, did it? What were some of the things you tasted? (Give time for responses.) When you put these all together they really make something delicious to eat. The finished product is worth it all.

"Things that happen in our lives are much like this lesson. (Read the scripture off the poster, emphasizing 'good.') Is everything in our lives good? Is it good to have a fire or to break a leg?

"Some things are very hard to understand and not a bit happy, but everything in our lives works for good when we love God. See if this poster will help you understand. Try to match things that happen to us with the ingredients in the cake." (Have list on right covered with strips until they guess. Discuss each individual event.)

Routine	tasteless most of time	water
Studies	causes us to squint	soda
Sickness/Accidents	sadness—hard to take	vinegar
Discipline	keeps us on our toes	salt
Special fun-things	vacations/parties	sugar
Disappointment	bitter but necessary	cocoa
Work	lots of it	flour
Friendships	many make life pleasant	vanilla
Love/concern for others	holds other things together	oil

"If we look at each of the events in our lives as part of a chocolate cake, it will help us understand why God allows them to happen. This week try to think of things that happen to you as an ingredient in the chocolate cake."

Song to Teach: "What a Friend We Have in Jesus," or "Take My Life."

The leader will need to have a chocolate cake made from the ingredients used in this lesson. This is the recipe for Crazy Chocolate Cake: 1-1/2 cups flour; 1/2 teaspoon salt; 1 teaspoon vanilla; 1 cup sugar; 6 Tbsp. oil; 3 Tbsp. cocoa; 1 Tbsp. vinegar; 1 teaspoon soda; 1 cup water. Mix together in one bowl. Pour into 9x13 cake pan. Bake 20-30 minutes at 325 degrees. Frost with fudge icing.

FOLLOWING JESUS

Scripture: Romans 8:28 — second program
   (continue to memorize this verse)
Story: "When we were children, my brother and I made up a game called 'Push.' We would play it for hours. When I was 'It' he would push me with a gentle shove wherever he wanted me to go. Sometimes it was into a mud puddle or over a log or into the barn or down a hill. Whenever I took extra steps on my own, then I lost and had to become a pusher.

   "Let's demonstrate this game. (Ask for a volunteer.) Now relax so you don't take your own steps. It's a silly game, isn't it? (Push across the front and back again.) I've noticed adults playing it, though.

   (Allow volunteer to be seated.) "Here's how they play: They pretend that they are 'It' and God is the pusher and that He is pushing them wherever He wants them to go. They get into trouble and expect God to push them out of it. Or if something goes wrong, they blame God for it. Sometimes they simply sit back and wait for God to push them hard to do this or that.

"Jesus told His disciples to follow Him. He's not a pusher, but a leader. He wants us to follow Him. He won't pull us or push us, but He will lead us.

"Last week we learned that not all things in life are easy or fun or good, but that put together right, they can become good—like the chocolate cake. God's plan for our lives will naturally involve some disappointments, and accidents. But as long as we love Him and are trying to fit into His plans, as the Bible says, everything will work out for good to those who follow Jesus."

Song to Teach: "Follow On."

WALKING IN THE LIGHT

(Younger children will not relate to this as will the older ones but they will need to be cultivated into these spiritual concepts. They'll enjoy talking about a flashlight and sharing if they have one. Their interest will be held).

Scripture: John 8:12 (memorize)

Sermon in a Sack—Object: Flashlight.

Hints: "This is something we really need at

night. (Pause for a guess or two.) It keeps us from tripping over a rock. (Ask) How many of you have a flashlight of your very own?" (Allow them to respond.)

While you listen to their conversation, take the batteries out and try to turn it on. Allow one of the younger ones to try to turn it on and ask him why it won't work.

"Jesus said, 'I am the light of the world; he that followeth me shall not walk in darkness, but shall have the light of life.' Jesus knew that He could lead people into a happy life. We can depend on Him.

"Occasionally, a flashlight won't work. This one happens to have new batteries and will work if we use them. Sometimes batteries wear out, though, and in the darkest moment we may have no light. (Elaborate about an experience in an electrical storm or camp-outs which some may have to relate.)

"Jesus said he could give us unending light. He is the only one who can. Some people depend on other people or things for light, but just like a dead battery, they won't work.

"Jesus is like a 'lifetime guaranteed battery.' In order to have this lifetime guaranteed light to happiness and to get to heaven too, we must give ourselves to Jesus when we're old enough to understand that He died on the cross in our place.

"Perhaps today is the day you understand this

and you want to give your life to Jesus." (Close in the way you choose.)

Song to Teach: "The Light of the World is Jesus"— second verse especially.

WORKING FAITH

(This will appeal more to older children who are beginning to reach out and serve the Lord.)

Scripture: Luke 8:43-48 (memorize Matthew 17:20)

Object Lesson: Use a lemon, an apple and a grapefruit. Explain that these fruits represent small, medium, and large ideas.

Story: "There was trouble at the underpass—great trouble. The cab of a diesel truck was stuck. The bridge was too low. Traffic was piling up while the truck driver and the highway patrolman discussed how to free the truck without damaging the new bridge or the expensive truck.

"Johnny, ten years old, had an idea as he watched from the roadside. But Johnny was timid about talking to the men. Finally, he got up courage and tugged on the officer's sleeve.

" 'Why not let a little air out of each tire, sir,' he stammered, 'and lower the truck enough to back it out?'

" 'Hmmmm, sounds like a good idea to me, son,' the officer said, and that is what they did.

"A little idea mixed with a little faith saved the day. Remember when King David was only a little boy with a little idea of aiming his sling-shot at the giant Goliath? That day he won a great battle with just a little faith, a little idea, and a little round stone. Of course, God was with him.

"There was a lady in Jesus' day who took a little idea, mixed it with a little more faith, and saw action too. Because of her sickness, no one was allowed to be around her. She was very unhappy and lonely. She felt that Jesus could heal her if she could only touch His garment. Sure enough, she was healed. Jesus wants us to mix what faith we have with ideas and ask His guidance. Then we can expect solutions to problems and answers to questions that we have.

"The Bible says in Matthew 17:20, *'If you had faith even as small as a tiny mustard seed . . . nothing would be impossible.'* We aren't born with a lot of faith but we do have enough to get started. If you say, 'I'll wait until I'm older so I'll have more faith to do something for God,' you might miss out doing something like what David did with the giant. God wants our faith to grow, and as it grows, He'll give us larger ideas.

"As we use our little lemon ideas and mix them with faith, God will give us apple ideas and then grapefruit ideas. As we work out solutions with His help, our faith will grow and we will have much happiness in serving God."

Song to Teach: "I Would be True."

WHAT IS SIN?

Scripture: Romans 3:23-24
    (memorize Romans 3:23-24)

Brainstorming: (Write answers on blackboard):
    "What is sin? lying? swearing? hitting? stealing? cheating?"

    "Are these the things that keep us from God? (Get responses.) Have you ever tried being good for an entire day? Did it work? (Responses.)

    "You have found out that it is impossible to be good for very long. Even mothers and daddies have a hard time being good all day long. Does that surprise you? It seems that no matter how hard we try, we can't stay out of trouble. Jesus knew this even before we were born, so He made arrangements for our sin problem. (Read the scripture from The Living Bible and off the poster.)

    "Jesus went to the source of our sin. What is the source? Did you ever watch a line of ants coming in the kitchen door after some sugar was spilled on the floor? You can kill them one at a time, but will that get rid of them? No, they keep coming. How do you get rid of them? (Allow response.) The way to do it is to get to the source. You must get to the beginning of the ant supply or you will be killing ants the rest of your life.

    "That's what sins are like. We can knock them off one at a time but they keep on coming.

We can quit lying for a day but find the next day it comes back. Sin is going our own way and that is the source of all the wrong things

SIN IS LIKE ANTS

we do. Just wanting to go our own way or do things our own way—without God's help—is the source of sin. It dates back to Adam and Eve in the Garden of Eden. Some people think that going your own way is the best way to have fun. Do what you want to do when you want to do it. That may sound like fun, and it may be fun for a while, but in the end it really isn't.

"It's like Pete who was going on a hike with a group of friends. He decided to go his own way because he thought the others wouldn't have much fun or walk fast enough. He saw some pretty things, but soon got lost and scared. After he realized he was unhappy and lost, he sat down on a log to think. He was so delighted when he heard voices coming near him. It was his group and he was glad to have his leader close by.

"We are all like that little Pete. We want to

go our own way but we need a leader. It's so much easier and more fun when you're with someone who knows where you are and where you're headed.

"Jesus is ready to forgive us too, for the sin of going our own way. He'll always be ready for us to follow Him. He forgives anytime a person asks Him to. Going our own way is always sinful, especially after we become Christians."

Songs to Teach: "Living for Jesus," "Follow On," or "I Know Where I'm Going."

INTRODUCING OTHERS TO JESUS

Scripture: John 15:14-15 (memorize)

Role play (choose your characters before worship):

Characters: John, Bob, and Rick (you play part of Rick, the spokesman)—no rehearsal is necessary.

"John, I want to tell you about my friend Bob. He's very special to me. He helps me with social studies and doesn't laugh when I fail spelling. Do you know him? (Wait for his response.)

"He helped me pick up books and papers the other day when someone knocked them off my desk. I'd sure like you to meet him. Would you be interested? (Wait for response.)

"He stands up for me when I get blamed for stealing things and he protects me when the bully gets after me. He listens to my long, drawn-out stories and doesn't say they don't sound true. I wish you could meet him sometime. He lives just down the street. Maybe you will run into him someday." (John will look blank.)

Questions: To the group—"Will Bob and John ever become friends? (Allow response.) It depends on a chance meeting. Does John know Bob after hearing all these things? (Allow response.) A person has to meet another personally—he only knows a lot about Bob. Let's change the scene and do it another way.

"John, you remember my telling you about Bob and all the ways he helps me? (Allow response.) I want you to meet him so badly that I'm going to take you to his house. He knows about you too. Want to go? (Allow John to respond. Then walk with him to the side of the room where Bob is standing.) John, meet Bob. (They shake hands and begin a dialog, previously suggested, about football or other sports, and go off together.)

"We must be like the Samaritan woman and bring our friends to meet Jesus. If you want your friends to meet Jesus, invite them to Sunday School and worship. Don't wait for them to come on their own; offer to pick them up."

Song to Teach: "What a Friend We Have in Jesus."

92

SPIRITUAL EYES

Scripture: 1 Corinthians 2:9

Poster: Montage of eyes (human, frog, snake, rabbit, eagle, cat, and any other kinds you can find).

Story: "One dark night when there was only a sliver of moon, a furry gray mouse hiding under a stack of wood watched a big red fox with a bushy tail creeping toward the barnyard where a red rooster was perched on a fence. What

did each of them see? The rooster saw only the sliver of moon. The mouse saw only a gray fox. The fox saw only a red rooster, and he was going to have him for a midnight snack.

"All eyes are made up of cones and rods that determine what we see. Cones enable an animal or person to see in the daylight. A rooster's eyes have all cones, and no rods, so he can see only in the light. This means he can't see at night unless the moon is bright. The mouse sees a gray fox because he has mostly all rods in his eyes. Like the fox and many other animals, he sees better at night. He doesn't see colors, though, but only black and white. Man has both cones and rods in his eyes but he has more cones. That's why we see better in the light and also see in color. Cats see very well at night because their eyes have rods.

"God has placed eyes in animals to suit the kind of life they live. An animal that is prey, or food, for another animal, like a rabbit, has eyes on the side of its head so he can eat or burrow while watching for other animals that are after him.

"A frog's eyes are set on top to permit him to watch where his enemy flies overhead, and swim and eat at the same time.

"An eagle's eyes have eight times better vision than man's because he scans the sky from miles above for food. Cats, who are predators to mice and rabbits, have forward eyes, like man, because they are equipped with claws and teeth for protection.

"God has certainly done a marvelous thing to provide just the right kind of eyes each animal needs. But I really want to talk about another set of eyes which humans can have, if they want them. Anyone want to guess? (They'll say 'telescope,' 'glasses,' etc.) These eyes never wear out. In fact, they get better and better the more one uses them. (Continue to hear guesses.)

"The Bible tells us about these eyes. (Someone may get it now. Read the verse.) These spiritual eyes help us understand others and to know what is the best thing to do. They help us find all the good and interesting things God has planned for our lives.

"Our way of life is meant to be spiritual, unlike animals whose lives are just survival. How good God is, to give us spiritual eyesight.

"So as persons, we see in daylight and a little at night, but even a blind person can have spiritual eyesight. Someday you'll read the story of Helen Keller, who was physically blind but saw many spiritual things.

"If you haven't received Jesus and the spiritual eyesight he has for you, you may do it today." (You may want to have a prayer and ask for decisions by raised hands.)

Song to Teach: "Open My Eyes" (all verses are excellent for children).

SERVE GOD

Scripture: 1 Corinthians 12:4-12

Story: (Adapted from story heard in a Children's Service many years ago.)

"Once a farmer found a strange little bird in his chicken coop. It was awkward and didn't look like a chicken at all but the farmer let it stay anyway. Soon the funny bird learned to eat and act just like a chicken, even though it still didn't look like one.

"Five years later when a friend was looking

over the chickens, he said, 'Why, that's not a chicken; it's an eagle!' He caught the little eagle and said to it, 'Look, you're not a chicken. You belong to the sky, not to the earth. Stretch your wings and fly high.' The eagle tried, but fell to the ground in a puff of dust.

"The man caught him again and again; each time he tried to get him to fly, but each time he failed. 'God has given you the ability to fly,' he kept saying. 'Now's the time to get your freedom.'

"Finally the eagle was successful and flew away. It soared off into the heavens, released to do what God had intended it to do. It never returned to the chicken coop because it finally began to act like an eagle.

"You are like that eagle. You belong to God and He's given you special abilities to do certain things. These are called talents, or gifts, and they can be used to serve God. Some people are content to 'scratch corn' with the chickens and are afraid to 'fly away' to do the things God has planned for them.

"Get ready to serve the Lord while you are young. Learn to play music, study, work, sing, worship, obey. All these things will help you find the special abilities God has given you."

Songs to Teach: "Take My Life and Let It Be," "Follow On," or "Trust and Obey."

COMMITMENT

(Use after eagle story)

Scripture: 1 Corinthians 12:4-12; Matthew 25:14-29

Object lesson: Flannelboard — pantomime combination.

Object: Glass jug with marble. Demonstrate centrifugal force by moving jug. Marble stays in jug as long as motion continues.

"The scripture says that God has given each person many things that he can do or learn to do. It takes a long time to master playing an instrument or studying to go through college, but God wants us to develop our abilities. It takes a lot of continuing motion to develop these abilities, like the jug and the marble. If you stop the motion, the marble stops.

"At your age you don't know what God wants you to do. It's your responsibility to try many things and find out what you like to do best and what your special abilities are. Unless we practice and use our abilities we may lose some of them. A story in the Bible that Jesus told illustrates this. I need three boys to pantomime." (Have signs flannel-backed for attaching to board later.)

SCENE 1: Matthew 25:14-18. (Have the boys take signs of $4,000, $2,000, and $1,000 as Scripture is read slowly from The Living Bible.)

SCENE 2: Matthew 25:19-29. (Owner returns and shows pleasure by giving $10,000 to the first boy and $4,000 to the second, but shows disappointment with the third by taking the original $1,000 and giving it to the first.)

"The owner wanted each man to use the money he gave him in the best way. This money stands for the talents God has given each of us. *He never by-passes anyone. Some may have more talents than others, but He expects us to use what we have in the best way we can.*"
Song To Teach: "Take My Life."

HEARING GOD SPEAK

Scripture: John 8:45 or Revelation 3:20
Game: Ask for a volunteer to sit behind a divider where there is a play phone. Then ask another volunteer to come to the play phone displayed

HEARING GOD

in front of the rest of the children and pretend to make a call to the first one.

The one behind the divider tries to identify the caller by voice, in addition to performing some act the caller suggests, like counting to ten, saying the ABC's, untying shoes, bending over, reciting a nursery rhyme or Bible verse. When the caller is identified, choose two new volunteers.

The object of the game is to illustrate that one person does not necessarily have to see another person in order to talk or receive orders.

"As Christians, God has given us things to do. How do we learn these things? (Wait for response: Bible reading, prayer, church attendance, what friends say—should all be mentioned.)

"We don't pick up a phone to get these instructions—God's way is even better than that. He uses parents, teachers, and friends to help us know what He wants us to do.

"First we must be willing to listen. Has anyone ever hung up on you on the phone? That's rude, but some people either hang up on God or don't even answer Him. He won't force a person to listen, but He never stops trying."

Songs To Teach: "I Can Hear My Savior Calling," or "Jesus Calls Us."

TALKING TO GOD

Scripture: John 11:22

Children read the following verses from slips of paper passed out or from their Bibles as assignments given out ahead of time:

Luke 18:1	John 14:14	John 15:7
Matthew 7:7	John 16:23	Mark 11:24

Brainstorming: Have one-word categories written
   on blackboard or poster:

Thankful	Say or do	Thankful
Help	Problems	Requests
Appreciate	Bible	

QUESTION 1: "For what are you thankful?" (Write
some response opposite "thankful"—they will
mention clothes, food, parents, and the like.)

QUESTION 2: "Whom do you know that has special
needs for God's help?" (Mrs. B.—ill, Jerry—
broken leg, minister, and the like.)

QUESTION 3: "Whom do you especially appreciate? (Sunday School teacher, mother, bus driver,
friend.) Now, answer these next questions in
your mind or silently."

QUESTION 4: "Did you do or say anything last
week that displeased God? Anything that you
were ashamed of? Did you steal? lie? curse?
sass? cheat?"

QUESTION 5: "Do you have problems getting along
with anyone in your family or neighborhood?
Do you tease, fight, or argue with anyone?"

QUESTION 6: "How did God help you last week?"
(They are still thinking of their answers silently.)

QUESTION 7: "Did you read the Bible and pray
any last week?"

   (After presenting these provocative questions
and allowing time to think, say "Amen.")

   "We were praying all this time with our eyes
open. That's what prayer is—being thankful for
God's provisions, appreciating people, being con-

cerned about others' needs, and also admitting our faults and seeing where we're wrong.

"Some people have the idea that they have to learn fancy words or be in church in order to pray. Some even think God is too busy to listen to them or that a problem has to be really serious before He will hear it.

"Some even believe that we have to be perfect in conduct before God will listen. If that were true, we wouldn't ever feel a need for God.

"We have several verses to read. After each has been read, decide where on our list they should go. (Have the verses read slowly and give oral applications, or let them think about where they apply.)

"God doesn't want us to keep our problems to ourselves or take His blessings for granted. He wants us to talk to Him just as we've talked here this morning."

Song to Teach: "Count Your Blessings."

STORIES TO PROMOTE CHRISTIAN GROWTH

NOTE TO LEADERS:

The next several lesson-story ideas were used with third through sixth graders. Since many of them have accepted the Lord, they need help in Christian growth.

The lessons on stewardship could be adapted

easily to younger children, since the true-life stories are quite simple and they do need to learn to give their offerings.

First a word about stewardship. In its widest meaning, this refers to giving a portion of time and talents, as well as money, to God and His church. In many churches, stewardship refers primarily to money, as it does in these lessons. Ordinarily a person who gives 10% of his income, or a significant portion, regularly to the church, gives his time and talent automatically.

One tends to support the organization to which he sacrificially invests his money. Since Jesus had much to say about giving money, I felt we should not neglect that emphasis with children.

Some churches teach tithing (giving 10%); some expect it; some insist on it and extract it. Other churches avoid it entirely but its members do practice regular giving.

We teach living by faith and use 2 Corinthians 9:7-8 as a basis for our attitude in giving. We feel 10% is a good place to begin.

I feel strongly that if a child learns while he is young to be generous with the Lord, his adult giving will follow as a matter of faith and trust also. Children love to give money to the Lord and will often give more sacrificially than adults.

We use faith-promise cards in our church, not only to encourage regular giving but to help everyone—even the children. Each person has a definite part in supporting God's work. We stress, however, that these promises are made to God and not to our church. No record is kept; the cards are destroyed after the amounts are tallied for budget purposes; and no bills are sent out.

There exists a close connection between a man's commitment and his pocketbook. We want our children to have the privilege of giving and understanding the basis for it from scripture.

GIVING TO GOD #1

Scripture: 2 Corinthians 9
    (memorize 2 Corinthians 9:7-8)
These verses are very important for a child to memorize, but it will take more than one Sunday to master the meaning. We used the same verses for all these lessons, spending four Sundays on them in all. Only a sample is presented in this book.
Story: "It was a lovely night to sled ride and all the kids in the neighborhood were out on the hill. Jimmy had a brand new sled he had never used and he was excited about the snow and getting to use his sled for the first time. He trudged up the hill with it and heard the other kids talk about his nice sled.

"Jimmy took one delightful ride and had a marvelous time. He walked briskly back up the hill. A bigger boy and his brother started to walk with him. 'We'd like to try your sled, kid.

Do you mind?' Jimmy didn't know what to say. He didn't know these boys.

"'I don't know,' he said, 'I've had only one ride.'

"'Aw, come on; don't be stingy.'

"'Yah, we'll see if it works all right,' the brother said.

"The big boys took the sled away from Jimmy.

"They took one ride . . . then another and another. Poor Jimmy stood at the top of the hill shivering and felt like crying.

"'I want my sled back!' Jimmy cried.

"'Just one more ride,' the bigger boy said. 'We've almost got it broken in.' The brothers just laughed.

"Down the hill they went. Jimmy watched them all the way. Finally they left his sled at the bottom of the hill and called to him. 'There's your sled, kid.' And they took off toward home with their broken-down sleds.

"How sad Jimmy was. He walked slowly down the hill to get his sled.

"Some people treat God just like that. They take God's things and act as though they own them. They use His gifts just for themselves and don't share them with Him. But everything belongs to God—our life, time, money, home, mind, family—everything we have is His.

"Though everything we have belongs to God, He won't take it without our wanting Him to. He waits until a person is willing to give it back to Him. He will not mistreat people and take more than they can give. As we see in our verses, He has promised to give us all our needs and then enough to share with our friends.

"Jesus is not thoughtless like those boys. He'll not leave us at the top of a hill, without a sled. But more than our money, God wants our hearts and our love. When we are willing to share what we have with God, that's a sign that we love Him—a sign that He has our hearts. It's not difficult to give to God when we love Him first."

Songs to Teach: "We Give Thee But Thine Own," "Trust and Obey," or "Bring Ye All the Tithes into the Storehouse."

GIVING TO GOD #2

Scripture Background: 2 Corinthians 9
   (continue memorizing verses 7-8)
Role Play (with a teenage helper): Adapted from "The Happy Giver" in MORE LITTLE VISITS WITH GOD (Concordia Pub., St. Louis).
   "If you had one million dollars, would you give some of it to Jesus? (The helper answers spontaneously.) If you had 400 dollars would you give part of it to Jesus? (Wait for his response.)
   "If you had ten dollars would you give one to Jesus? (Pause.) "If you had one dollar would you give part of it to Jesus?" (The teenager

may struggle here about not having much left over if he gave part of only one dollar.)

To the group: "It's easy to say we'd give a lot of something if we didn't have it. But Jesus wants us to look at what we have and share it cheerfully. Today we'll look at Mr. Lakes. He's willing to give, but he has problems."

Object Lesson-Story-Discussion:

Line up ten apples (or potatoes) on a table. Say, "These represent Mr. Lakes' weekly income. To make it easy and simple, let's say each stands for $10. How much does Mr. Lakes make in a week? (Wait for response.)

"He spends two apples on rent (have volunteer remove two apples) . . . one for food . . . one on insurance . . . two for the light bill. The telephone needs one. How many has he used? He has four left. The gasoline bill comes—there go two more. His son, Bill, needs a new winter coat—that's another one. How many are left? Just one. What should he do with the last of his pay? (Receive responses: they may say going to a movie, eating out, saving, and some may even mention giving to church.)

"Mrs. Lakes suggests they give some to church. Mr. Lakes agrees and says he will give a little. On Saturday, however, he has car trouble and it takes the last $10 to get it fixed.

"Every week is the same. There never seems to be much, or any, left for church. How much of Mr. Lakes' income does God want? (Receive responses—some children may know about tithing or giving regularly. Write the word 'Tithing' on the board. Pronounce it and ask who knows what it means.)

"The Jews had to give 10% of their belongings to God. Some churches today expect or make their members give 10%, whether they want to or not. All we have belongs to the Lord, so we do need to know what we should give back to Him. We don't believe we are forced to give 10% to the Lord, but it's a good amount to start with.

"How much would Mr. Lakes give if he gave 10%? Only $10.00 a week. He could start by giving $5.00 until he worked up to $10.00. Many people give a lot more than 10%.

"Let's put the apples back on the table and start Mr. Lakes' week over again." (Repeat the bills that come in and take his money. Never have any left over. Repeat several times until someone suggests taking the $10 for God out first and waiting until another week to buy a coat or buy new furniture.)

Song to Teach: One on giving.

GIVING TO GOD #3

Scripture: 2 Corinthians 9:7-8, continued
Brainstorming:
"How many of you receive an allowance? How

many have jobs you get paid for? What do you spend it on?

"I want to tell you about Jerry. He's eleven years old and gets $1.00 a week. He makes extra sometimes when he does special jobs. I'm putting ten jelly beans on the table to represent what Jerry makes . . . each jelly bean is worth how much?

"On Monday Jerry bought a candy bar and coke . . . that took 30 cents. (Let someone remove three jelly beans.) Tuesday he called home from the pay phone at school . . . he forgot his gym bag. Another 10 cents. On Thursday, lunch was poor so he bought ice cream to fill up—another 10 cents gone. Friday night was movie night—admission was 50 cents. He was down to 10 cents—better save that for Sunday School.

"Saturday, after his chores were done, he and his friend John went for a bike ride. It was pretty hot. 'Boy, I'm thirsty,' John said. 'You got money for cokes?' 'I have only one thin dime,' Jerry replied. 'I've got a nickel,' John added. 'We have enough to split a coke.'

"Jerry hesitated but he was really thirsty. There went his last dime. Sunday morning came. 'Mother, I need money for church,' Jerry said. 'Where's your allowance?' 'It's gone—I spent it.' His mother gave him a quarter, but it wasn't *his* gift to God.

"Let's go over Jerry's week again. (Repeat as for Mr. Lakes, using signs for things Jerry would buy. They will suggest he take his church dime out first and not carry it in his pocket. Go over 2 Cor. 9:7-8, and again, when it says, 'have enough left over to give cheerfully to others,' allow each child to put his hand in a sack and get a jelly bean.)

"If as a child you learn to take out your gift for God first, then when you become a father like Mr. Lakes, it will be easy to have plenty to give to the Lord and support His work. It's hard to learn to give after you are grown up."

Ask a layman, preferably a tither, to tell briefly how God has blessed him by his giving systematically.

Present giving as a happy privilege rather than a "better give it first before God takes it from you" attitude.

Song to Teach: Carry out the theme of giving.

GIVING TO GOD #4

Scripture: 2 Corinthians 9:7-8

I am including this dialog with our puppets, who are regular visitors in our Children's Worship, not so much to be used as a program in the church but to show how easy it is to write conversations discussing scripture and informing kids about things they need to know. Zip and Zap also help set attitudes and really keep the attention of the children. We tape the voices—children work the puppets.

Zip: "Well, Zap, it looks like we've learned everything about stewardship and what it means to give to God."

Zap: "I don't know about everything, Zip. The more you grow as a Christian, the more you'll learn about giving. It gets real tough sometimes to give to God."

Zip: "I didn't have a bit of trouble this week. My mom was impressed that I got my own Faith-Promise Card in the mail. It's fun to give my own money rather than my mom's."

Zap: "Hope you explained that to her right."

Zip: "I think I did . . . she said some churches are always asking for money, but I explained to her that if Christians gave what God wanted them to, no one would have to mention it."

Zap: "You are partially right, Zip. But as long as we have new Christians, and I hope that's all the time, we're going to have to teach the importance of giving just like we teach loving. It's part of our life of faith—even if the church didn't need money."

Zip: "I do have one question, Zap. I put down on my card 20 cents a week. I make $2.00, you know, and I wonder—what if I make $5.00 some week? What would I put in? I want to keep the records straight."

Zap: "A good question, Zip. You'd give at least 50 cents or whatever you believe God wants you to give."

Zip: "Won't that get my record messed up?"

Zap: "Oh, no. Those cards are burned as soon as they get the total amount for budget purposes. No one ever checks up to see if you give what you wrote down. It's a promise between you and God. No one else even knows what it was. Let me ask you a question."

Zip: "Make it easy, please."

Zap: "What if you're sick one week—then what do you do about giving?"

Zip: "Guess I'll be 20 cents ahead in my savings . . . no . . . I can tell that was the wrong answer . . . ah, let me see . . . hmmm . . . bring it the next week?"

Zap: "I'll buy that last answer. If you can't send it with someone, bring it the next week."

Zip: "What if recession hits . . . even me? Say I don't make $2.00?"

Zap: "Then you have to give what you think God would have you give. That's where living faith comes in. The verse says He will provide your needs if you give cheerfully and I've found out that He keeps His promise. I have always been able to give at least 10% of my income, and many times I go over. I've always had enough for my needs and enough left to share with others. It works."

Zip: "I'm going to give 30 cents next week and see what happens."

Zap: "I can promise you'll be blessed. He won't necessarily return your money but you'll probably get another opportunity to make some more money and have the chance to help someone, and that will bring more happiness.

Zip: "See you next week."

LESSON-STARTER SUGGESTIONS

These ideas are included to give a director or leader a start in writing his own material. First choose the theme. (It may be a subject needing a scriptural basis or a parable or story from the Bible needing application.) Then learn how to go from the known to the unknown, for that is the mechanics of teaching children abstract ideas which form the basis of their life-decision process. These are seed ideas for going from a subject to abstract teaching with vehicles to aid in the transition.

Let's say our purpose is to impress the children that God will speak to them. How do we go from the known to the unknown? First, after we have looked over several scriptures referring to the subject, we begin to think about some tangible object related to hearing, something that we have to plug in to or turn on. There could be earplugs, radio, television, or telephone.

Would an object lesson, little story, or montage get the children most quickly from the truth of God speaking to us and the reality or proof that He does? The lesson on "Hearing God" is an example of how I presented this truth. There are many other ways, one of which anyone could teach well.

Let's say our scripture is chosen first, like 1 John 1:9. The subject is forgiveness of sin. The word "cleanse" will say something tangible to a child. Any object can be put into a sack for a little guessing beforehand—to capture interest. For example: "I have something in my sack today that everyone uses. (Pause.) Boys about ten years of age usually have to struggle to use it. (Pause.) We should use it before eating. The Bible says God will cleanse us in a different way." Continue with your idea. You've gotten them interested.

Another one on 1 John 1:9 could start like this: "I'm used every day. (Pause.) I have only one purpose. Girls like me especially. (Pause.) I always tell the truth and people believe me. Sometimes I'm in a girl's purse, sometimes on a wall, but nearly always in the bathroom." They will have guessed mirror by now. Go on to say, "God's Word is like a mirror. We all see in it how much we need Jesus to help make our lives beautiful."

Then continue with the thought according to the needs of your groups. Using a hymn like "Open My Eyes" or "Let Others See Jesus in You" would help. Write out your verse to memorize, and your program is formed.

Soon you will be able to go from scripture truth, parables, or Bible stories to whatever application you wish to make for your children. Variety is the key to interest. It takes practice and prayer.

One must guard against taking the analogies in parables too far and teaching more truths than Jesus intended to in the first place. He moved from the known to the unknown but was careful to stop before getting too involved in the comparisons.

In the lesson ideas that follow, the scriptures, stories, objects, and songs are only suggestions. There are many other possibilities available to the leader who will open his or her mind to God's creativity. These are just the beginnings. The rest is up to you.

OUR MINDS

Scripture: Proverbs 23:7
Sermon in a Sack—Object: Soap

Hints: "Pretend this bar is our mind. Everything we hear, do, or think impresses our minds. (Make a scratch with a nail. Show them the imprint. Then tell a story about the third grader who heard a dirty story at school. Just hearing it made a little impression—demonstrate. Then he tried to remember it—this made more of an impression—demonstrate. He repeated it to his brother—a deeper impression.) We are the guards of our minds. Be careful what you listen to or see."

STRAIGHTENED LIVES

Scripture: 2 Corinthians 5:17
Object: Nail and pliers
Application: "Sometimes carpenters pull bent nails from old wood to use again. (Bend the nail.) The nails have to be straightened first. (Try to straighten.) It's very difficult to straighten this nail. It's not the way it was before. Our lives get bent and out of shape. Only God can straighten them."

Naturally, this one would be for children who are old enough to make moral choices and are realizing the claims of Jesus on their lives and their need to accept Him.

KEEP LIFE IN TUNE

Scripture: Romans 12:1-2
Make up story about a concert pianist who walks on stage and sits before a huge piano. Crowd cheers . . . everything gets quiet. He begins . . . then stops. He begins again and

stops. He stands before the audience and sorrowfully tells them he can't go on. There's a key out of tune. Proceed to say why he can hear it but others can't.

"The Master is aware of every sour note in our lives. A piano doesn't need waxing but does need a tuner. People attempt to cover sour notes with smiles, words, and good deeds, but they need a tuner. God is our tuner."

An excellent song after this story is "He Keeps Me Singing." This, also, is for older children the way it's presented here. It could, however, be modified and used with younger children.

WE NEED GOD'S WORD

Scripture: John 3:16
Object: Leaf
Application: "This leaf needs two things in order to function. It must be fastened to a tree (salvation) and it needs sunlight (growth through prayer, Bible reading, and fellowship). We get God's power by accepting His Son." Again for older children.

FORGIVENESS

Scripture: 1 John 1:9 (Another lesson on 1 John 1:9)
Object: Egg
Hints: "This is something we have for breakfast; use in potato salad . . . (Then tell story of

Humpty Dumpty. Drop the egg, which is in a plastic bag.) It cannot be fixed.... (Finish story with "All the King's horses and all the king's men. . . .") When we commit sin, the laws that God gave are broken and can't be repaired. But God can fix things after we have lied or stolen or gone our own way. He forgives and gives us a chance to improve. We must ask Him." For older children.

TELL OTHERS

Scripture: Matthew 6:33
Object: Picture of someone they know
Application: "You can tell by his features who it is. How can we convince another person that God is real? Telling others about it is one way; the way we act is another. We need to live in such a way that people get the picture of God. Others will know that we have met Jesus and talk to Him every day." "Let Others See Jesus in You" is a good hymn.

OBEDIENCE

Scripture: Romans 6:13
Object: Pencil and paper
Hints: "This is something we use at school. (Demonstrate good and poor writing.) The pencil obeys the writer. It could write very beautifully if the right person had it. So our lives, in the

hands of the right person, can be beautiful. As long as we go our own way, our lives are poor, but let Jesus control us through scripture and prayer, and our lives become beautiful." For older children, or those who have become Christians, to see the importance of growth.

SALVATION

Scripture: John 14:6
Object: Blank check
Hints: "I have something in my sack today that many parents use on bill-paying day. (Give several hints.) In order to be used it must be properly filled out and signed by the right person. Jesus is the only person who can get us to God. When He died on the cross, it was like signing His name on our behalf."

CHARACTER

Scripture: 2 Corinthians 4:4 or Revelation 3:17
Object: Glasses (blinders on them)
Application: "Just like the blind man Jesus healed, we are all blind until we meet Christ personally. It is not enough to hear about Him or read about Him. We must meet Him and see Him individually. Then we can talk to Him ourselves. It will all be clear."
Hints: "This is something we need in school for

math and also in art classes. An inch is always an inch, whether you're measuring pipe or lace. It stays the same through the ages—just like the Bible. The Ten Commandments are a good rule. They never change."

HABITS

Scripture: Philippians 4:8-9
Object: Thread
Hints: "I need a strong boy to help me. Hold out both hands while I wrap a few strands of thread around them. Think you can snap these threads? Sure you can. Now, let's wrap a few more. (Use enough so he won't be able to break them.) This illustrates habits. The more you develop them, the harder they are to break, whether they be good habits or bad habits."

THE WAY WE ARE MADE

Scripture: Psalm 139:14
Object: A watch
Hints: "Most people wear one of these. It keeps us on time. It is very intricately made and the least bit of dust slows it down or makes it stop. It must be accurate to be any good. We must keep it clean. We can't help others unless we're truthful and what we say and do is on target. Others are always watching what we do and trying to get direction from us or copy us."

GUIDE

Scripture: John 14:6

Object: A map

Hints: "This is something we need on a trip or in a new city. The Bible is our map to God, but it is only a guide. You could memorize a map and still not get where you wanted to go. No one gets to the Father except through His son, Jesus. Knowing verses or going to church does not automatically get us to God."

GOD'S WORD

Scripture: James 2:10

Object: A ruler

LESSON IDEAS FROM PARABLES

Parables are earthly stories with heavenly meanings that Jesus told. They each have one main teaching and are excellent examples of going from the known to the unknown. It is good to study and use Jesus' methods of teaching. Some of the thirty-two or so parables are too deep for children. We used the following series with third-sixth graders, always going from the known to the unknown.

LOST SHEEP

Scripture: Luke 15

Go from modern story to parable. Make up a story about a child who got lost at the fair or at a department store. Tell how his parents searched. Pick out names; tell through conversation how the child felt, how the parents felt, where they looked, what they did. Emphasize their joy in finding the child. A leader could tell the story, or puppets could be used to present it.

After this story, let the children read scripture (about the Lost Sheep) or listen to it read aloud. Emphasize again how the shepherd and his friends rejoiced—and that just so, when a person accepts Christ, there is rejoicing, or should be, by all who know the Lord.

THE SOWER

Scripture: Luke 8:4-18
Poster: Show different types of ground: trampled,

ALLOW CHILDREN TO HELP

rocky, thorny, and fertile (include a bird in the air). Go from the known to the unknown: what would happen if a seed fell on each? Then proceed with scripture and compare ground to different types of hearts.

NOTES

NOTES

NOTES

NOTES

NOTES

NOTES

NOTES